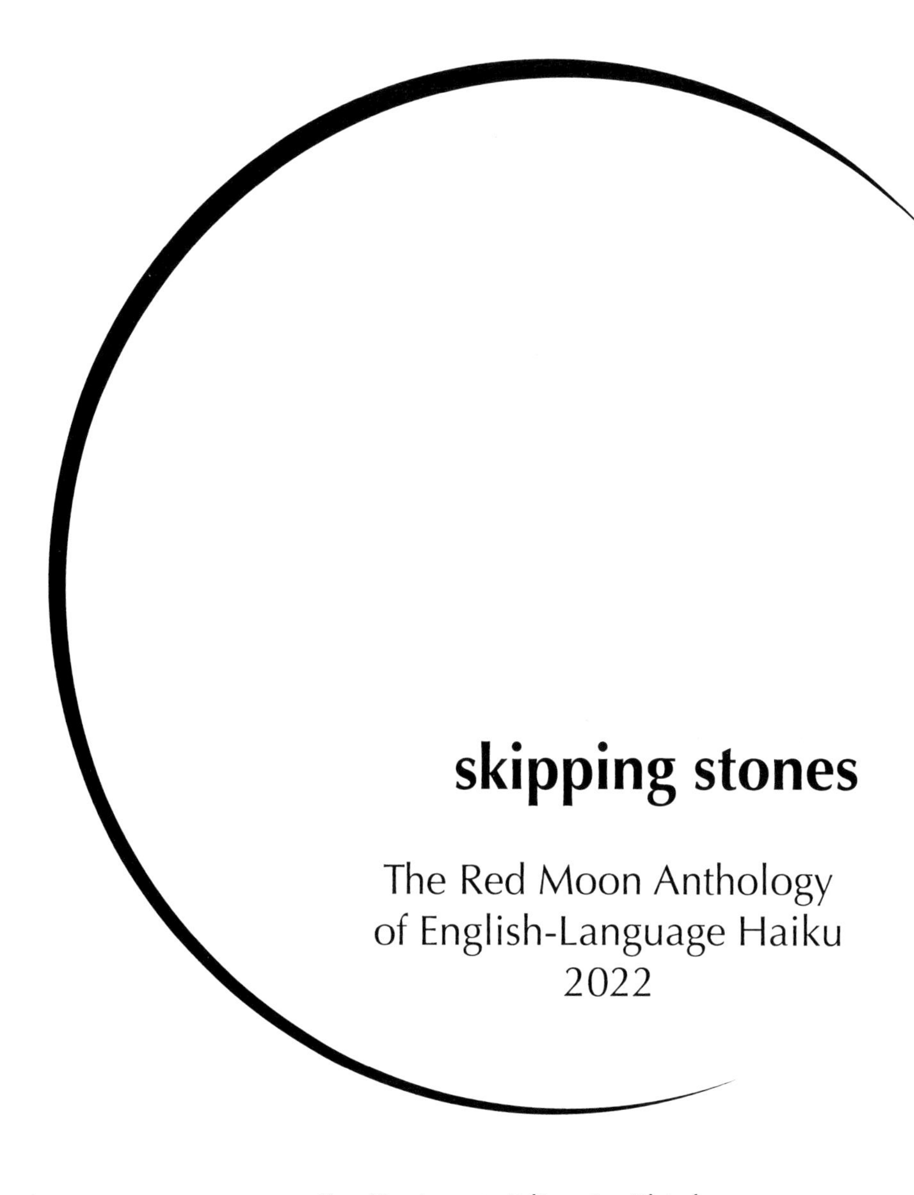

skipping stones

The Red Moon Anthology of English-Language Haiku 2022

Jim Kacian ✧ Editor-in-Chief

Francine Banwarth ✧ Randy M. Brooks
LeRoy Gorman ✧ Maureen Gorman
Gary Hotham ✧ David Jacobs
Tomislav Maretic ✧ David McMurray
Julie Schwerin ✧ Sandra Simpson

skipping stones

The Red Moon Anthology of English-Language Haiku 2022

First Printing

Published by
Red Moon Press
P. O. Box 2461
Winchester VA
22604-1661 USA
www.redmoonpress.com

ISBN 978-1-958408-16-2

Special thanks to Sandra Simpson,
proofreader *extraordinaire*, and to
Marta Chocilowska, internet maven.

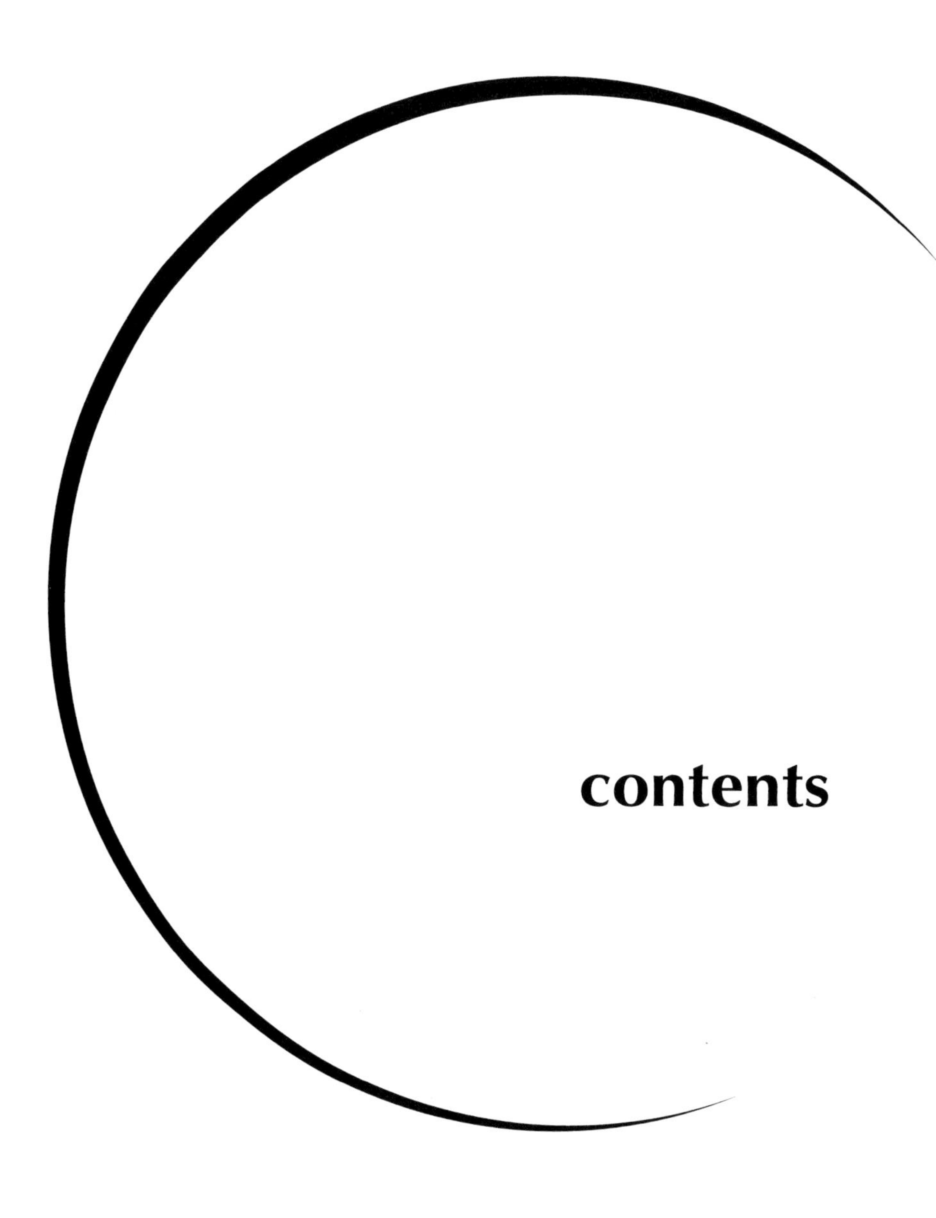

contents

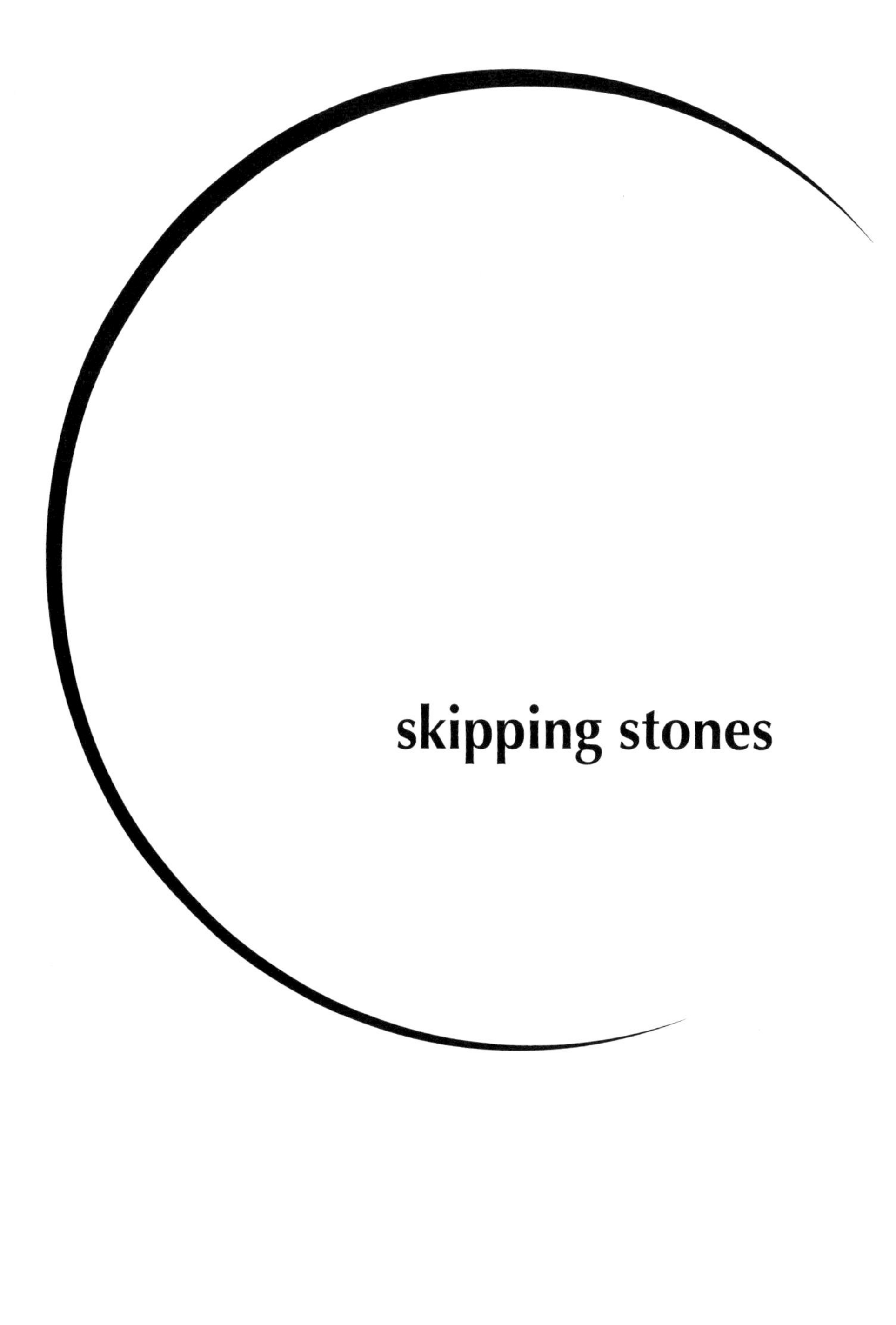

skipping stones

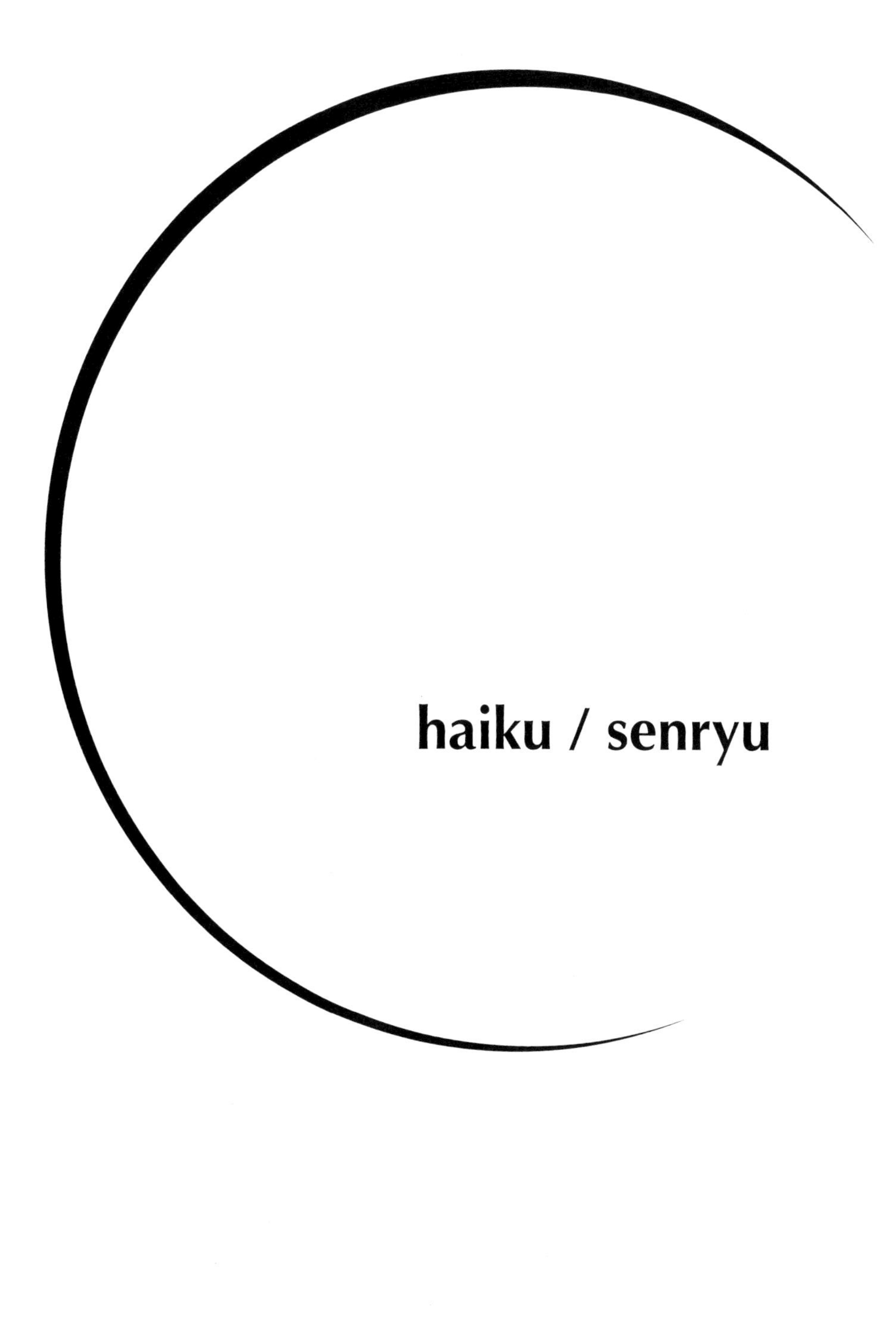

haiku / senryu

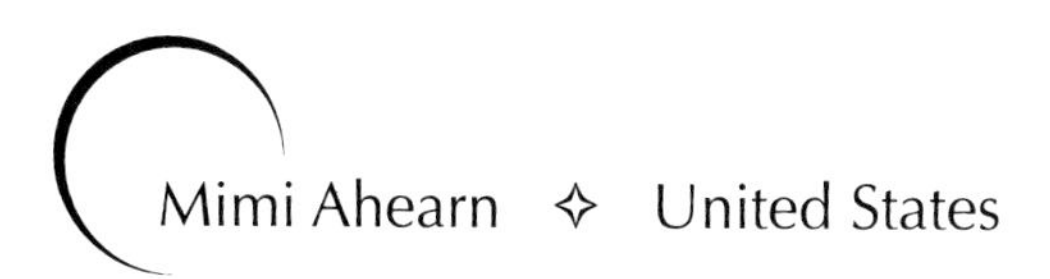

Mimi Ahearn ✧ United States

until I hear
otherwise . . .
birdsong

Ramesh Anand ✧ India

summer solstice
the last marathoner gets
the longest hurray

after all her sisters wore it first communion dress

airport taxi . . .
all the reasons
leave with her

Susan Antolin ✧ United States

uncut pomegranate —
the private things
she knows I know

night wind —
the sound of leaves
not letting go

the year ending —
I turn off lights
in empty rooms

Marilyn Ashbaugh ✧ United States

jumping the gun summer heat

Hifsa Ashraf ✧ Pakistan

night in a forest
feeling the pulse
of every tree

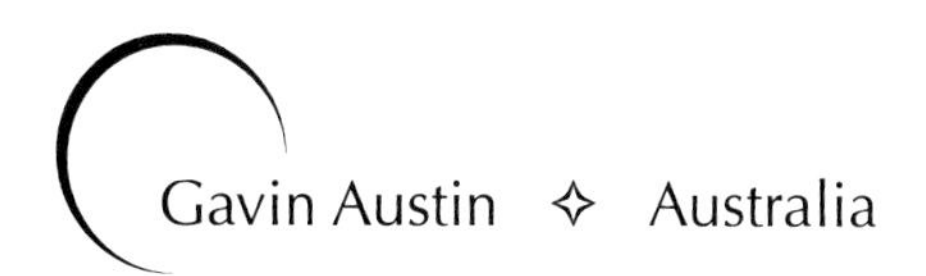

Gavin Austin ✧ Australia

again he checks
his packed bag
the shared child

Stewart C. Baker ✧ United States

an old pond . . .
nothing to account
for the ripples

trying to excavate the owl from my father's well of forgetfulness

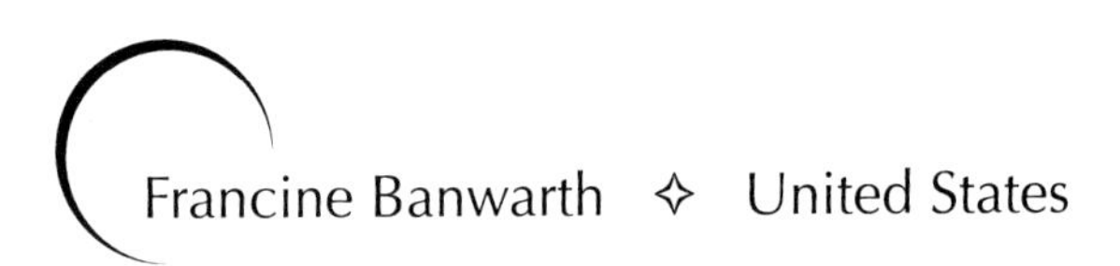

newborn's death date no wind to speak of

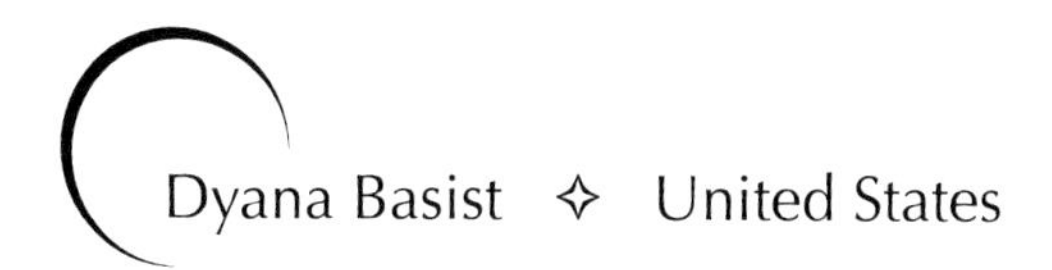

Dyana Basist ✧ United States

mother's day
shaking a pebble
from her shoe

Royal Baysinger ✧ United States

not there
to remind me who's who
—your funeral

Roberta Beary ✧ United States/Ireland

forsythia
the pallbearers
reassemble

Mona Bedi ✧ India

pandemic
gradually I become
the oldest

the sky without a prescription

an apology . . .
the predictive text
writes it for me

Steve Black ✧ United Kingdom

call to prayer
a half-eaten apple
on the garden path

Kathryn Bold ✧ United States

divorce papers
only our signatures
haven't changed

a stone child
clings to a stone skirt
temple ruins

dark side of the moon
we'll get around
to it

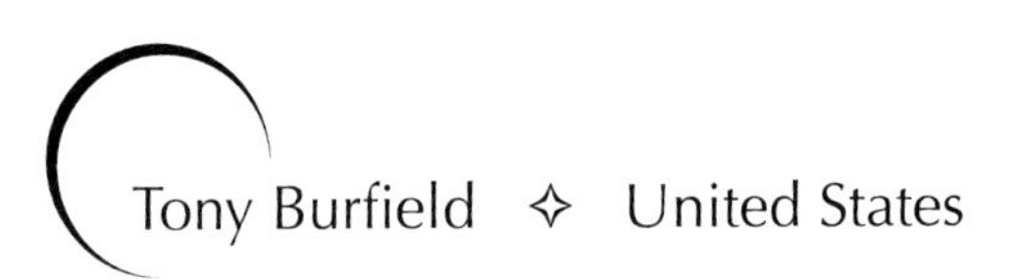

marriage breaking the jigsaw puzzle back to pieces

afternoon moon
she opens her set
of soft pastels

Christopher Calvin ✧ Indonesia

skipping stones
answering questions
with questions

Claire Vogel Camargo ✧ United States

covid moon
attaching her
first toe tag

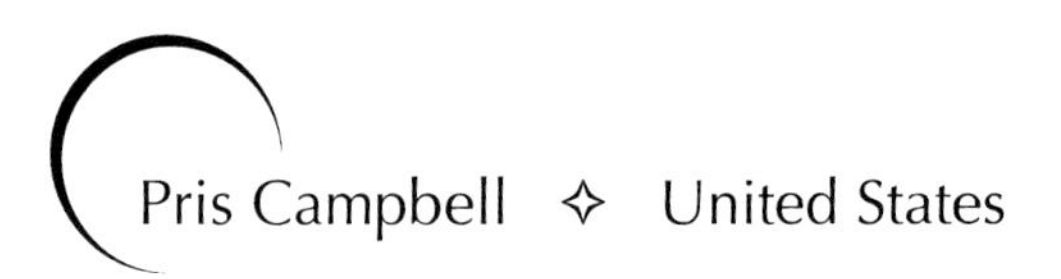

Pris Campbell ✧ United States

window shopping
my reflection tries on
every dress

Liam Carson ✧ Ireland

a murmuration of snow
in the street light . . .
souls of the departed

Paul Chambers ✧ Wales

a child's drawing
sellotaped to a headstone
april wind

Salil Chaturvedi ✧ India

accompanying our dog
into the grave —
robin's song

Antoinette Cheung ✧ Canada

after the night shift
the soft thud
of her car door

Satyanarayana Chittaluri ✧ India

climate change
now she says
no

Florin C. Ciobîcă ✧ Romania

mayfly nymph
she begins to speak about
that miscarriage

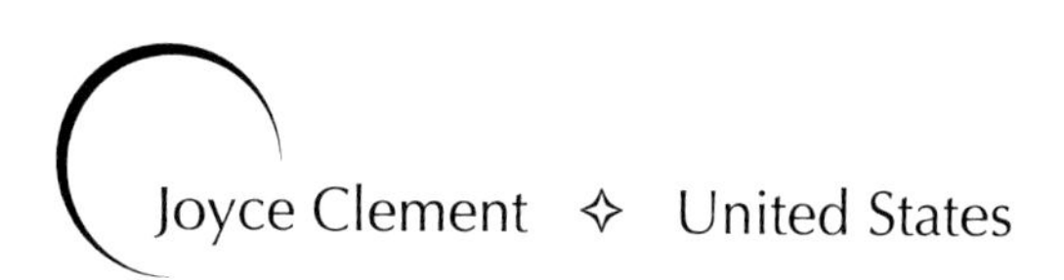

Joyce Clement ✧ United States

retirement
most of my i’s
left undotted

Glenn G. Coats ✧ United States

enough to cover the cross   river mist

Stephen Colgan ✧ United States

drinking alone
I sift through the shells
for the last pistachio

Sue Courtney ✧ New Zealand

night migration the moon and the moon and the moon

Alvin B. Cruz ✧ Philippines

my assigned gender violets are blue

binge watching the waves roll in

amaryllis wombs no longer their own

Frank Dietrich ✧ Germany

i am i am not the darkness between subway stations

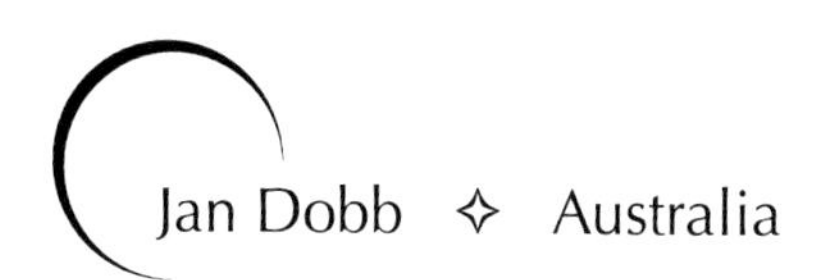

Jan Dobb ✧ Australia

rural dawn
every long shadow
ends at a cow

Rebecca Drouilhet ✧ United States

winter tree
one of us
looks good naked

Michael Dudley ✧ Canada

muddy March
their crop field plowed
by soldiers' boots

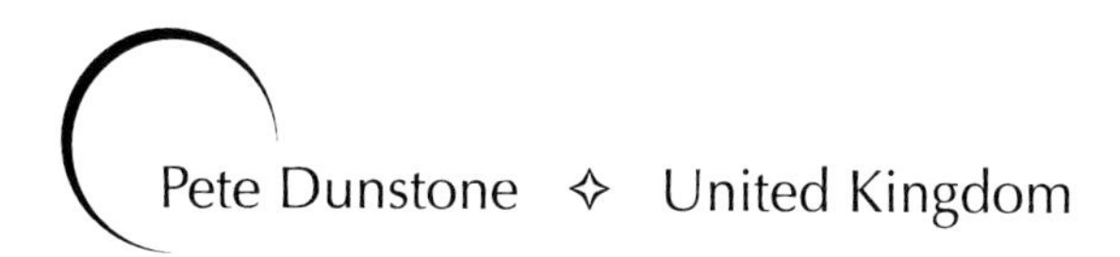
Pete Dunstone ✧ United Kingdom

winter bonfire
the old diaries
slow to burn

Baisali Chatterjee Dutt ✧ India

blood moon
an almost-life trickles
down my legs

Anna Eklund-Cheung ✧ United States

mist on the river . . .
the Christmas day stroll
before their return flights

Paul Engel ✧ United States

two-day bus ride
to dad's funeral —
mountains are just mountains

Keith Evetts ✧ United Kingdom

autumn leaves the things we can't

David Kawika Eyre ✧ United States

compost
the eternity
of circles

Ignatius Fay ♦ Canada

the moment I know
I've gone too far
freezing drizzle

P. H. Fischer ✧ Canada

old ghosts —
i buy 'em all
a stiff drink

pitting the figurative against the literal old hat

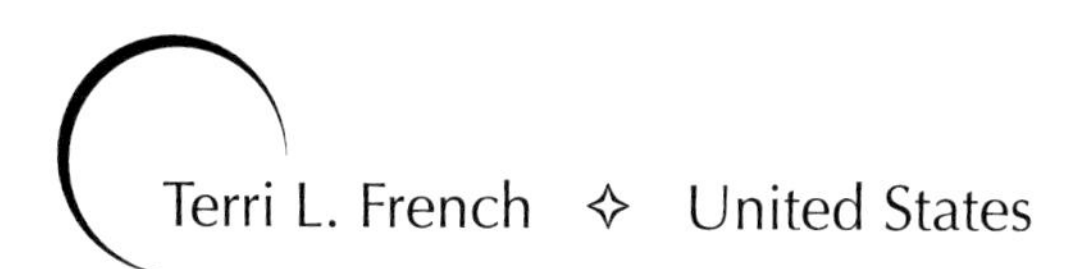

counseling session
we always start
with the weather

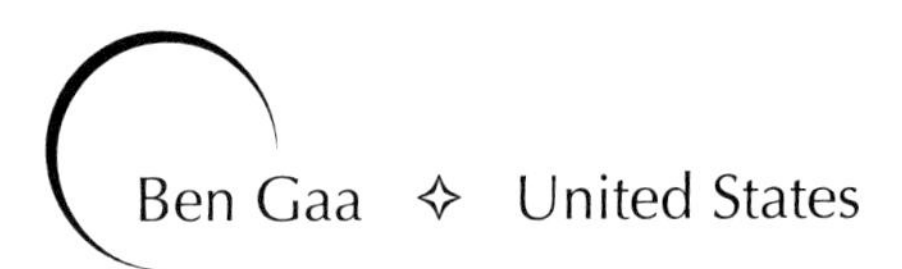

growing smaller
in my hand
my mother's

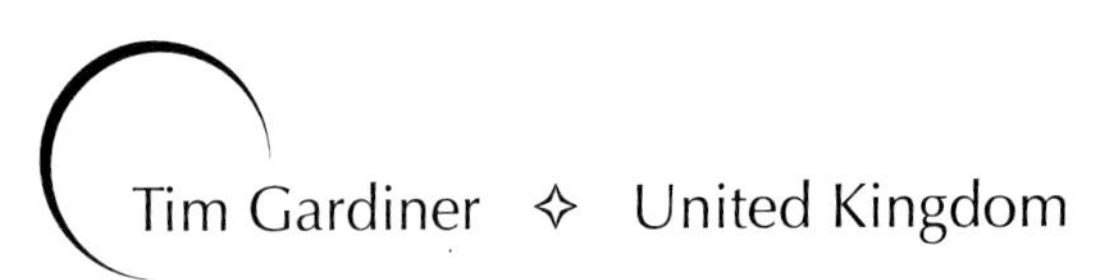

when there's no one left
to tend your grave
starlight

family reunion . . .
mother's photo
maintaining order

custody hearing
in full view
a melting snowman

Benedict Grant ✧ Canada

your lawyer
handing me his pen
summer's end

prison gardener
sometimes it's the soil
he says

Lee Gurga ✧ United States

catch
and release
a father's love

Ian Tracy Gwin ✧ United States

flecks of spring rain —
a mourner speaks with me
in present tense

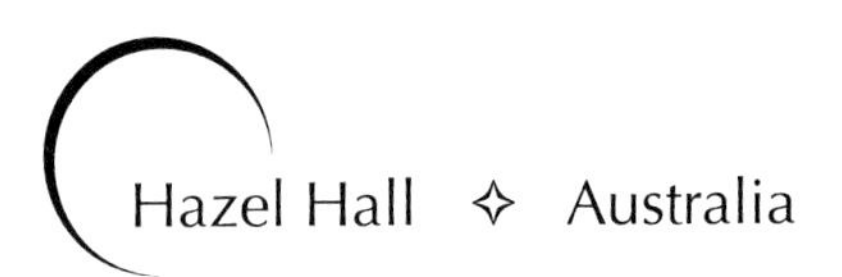

Hazel Hall ✧ Australia

finding a way
to live with her loss
melting snow

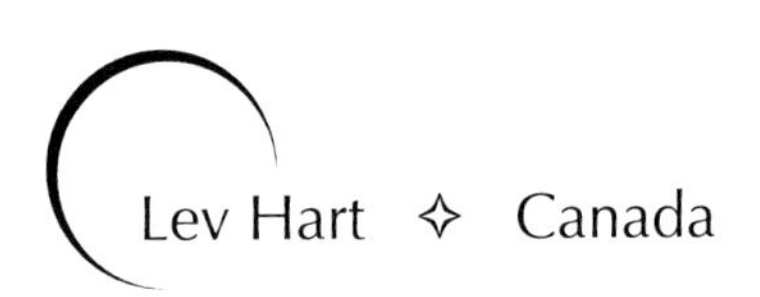

Lev Hart ✧ Canada

a woman   unbuttoning   spring

Ruth Holzer ✧ United States

sharing
what little there is —
winter finches

Frank Hooven ✧ United States

stray dog
the long day
follows me home

Gary Hotham ✧ United States

whatever
the rain decides
the river takes

louder
in parts of the room
the memory

news
we haven't heard
the brook finds its way past us

Edward Cody Huddleston ✧ United States

new therapist
I explain
the kigo

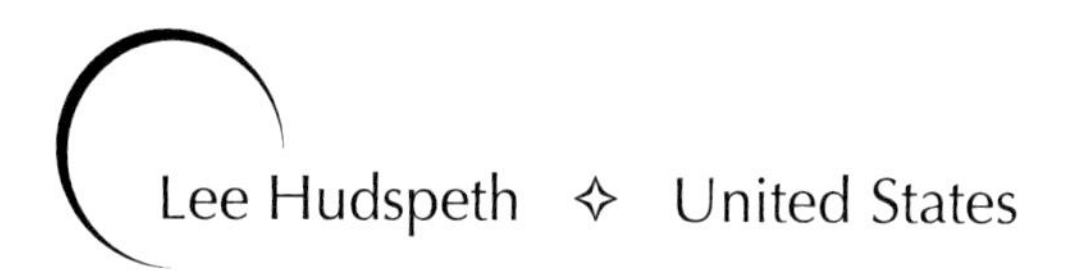

Lee Hudspeth ✧ United States

kayak river tour
the kingfisher
everyone else saw

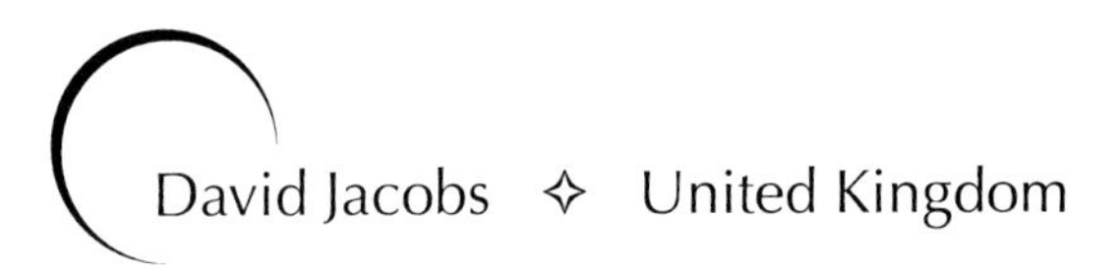

David Jacobs ✧ United Kingdom

low winter sun
my shadow reaches the grave
long before me

Roberta Beach Jacobson ✧ United States

metal bracelet
my condition has
a name

Jim Kacian ✧ United States

a last scattering of birds at dusk these late poems

tracking your path
by the lights you turn on
firefly

scars from scrapes i don’t recall indian summer

William Keckler ✧ United States

Auschwitz tourists —
all day a loose button
on the ground

David J. Kelly ✧ Ireland

burnt forest
another dawn
without its chorus

Julie Bloss Kelsey ✧ United States

rising fog
unwrapping
the city

Bill Kenney ♦ United States

careful what I wish for one more spring

Susan King ✧ United Kingdom

slow afternoon . . .
the cat decides at last
to wash the other ear

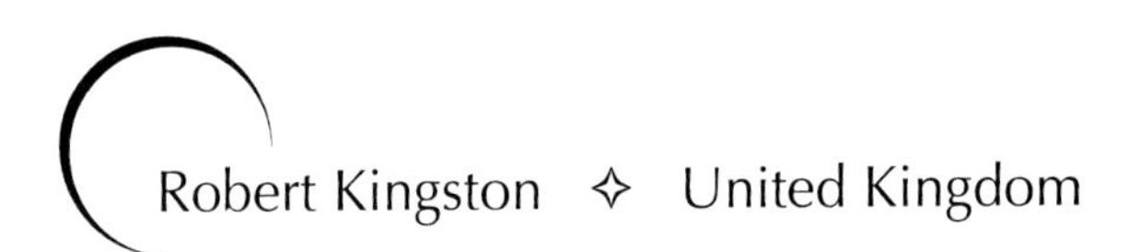

Robert Kingston ✧ United Kingdom

identity crisis I tick both boxes

Jessica Malone Latham ✧ United States

bone moon
picking through
hand-me-downs

Jim Laurila ✧ United States

family reunion
she slips into her
childhood accent

tai chi
again
i stand corrected

spring cleaning
re-taping the box
of old diaries

Kristen Lindquist ✧ United States

green blackberries . . .
explaining again
our right to choose

April wind unloosing the spring in her hair

a long letter
from the new widow
hunger moon

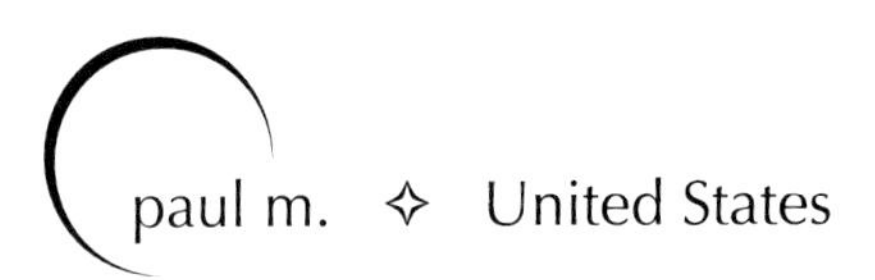

paul m. ✧ United States

mother's room . . .
its darkness contains
a mirror

suspecting mine
is the placebo . . .
January moon

Patricia J. Machmiller ✧ United States

the magnolia
wasn't ours, yet its absence
is

Carole MacRury ✧ United States

used book
finding my alter ego
in the margins

before the rain
the smell of rain
morning of her due date

Mom's labored breath
we sit on the seawall
to watch the waves

Catherine Mair ✧ New Zealand

brief obituary
he didn't
like a fuss

Annette Makino ✧ United States

Covid variant
another wave sucks the sand
from under our feet

dusty cloud —
a herd of hooves
passes along the country road

my life and times new roman

Scott Mason ✧ United States

snowmelt
the church carillon
changes its tune

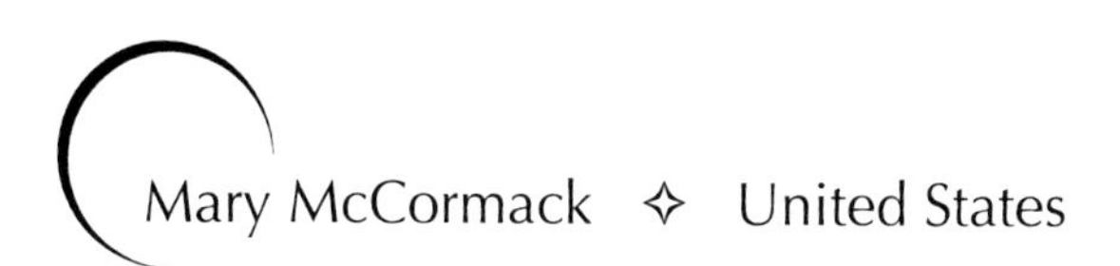

Mary McCormack ✧ United States

brushstrokes
her shape
in his hands

Tanya McDonald ✧ United States

encrypted snow the fox sparrow's password

Marietta McGregor ✧ Australia

epitaph
the white noise
of surf

Dan McKinley ✧ United States

new year calendar
compliments of
the funeral home

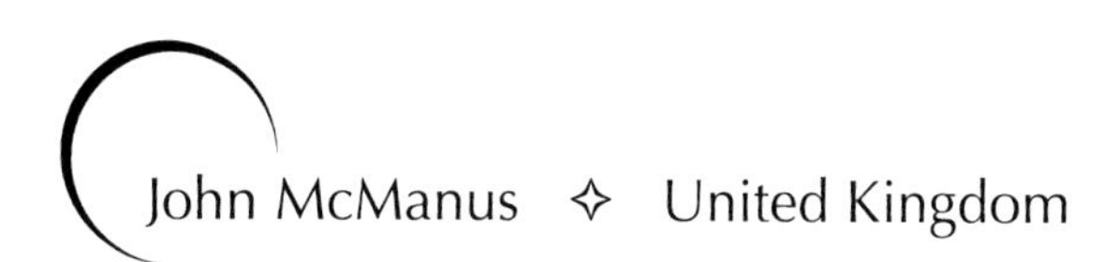

John McManus ✧ United Kingdom

night light
Mother asks me
to leave it on

David McMurray ✧ Canada/Japan

light echoes across
the wings of a male godwit
springtime sun

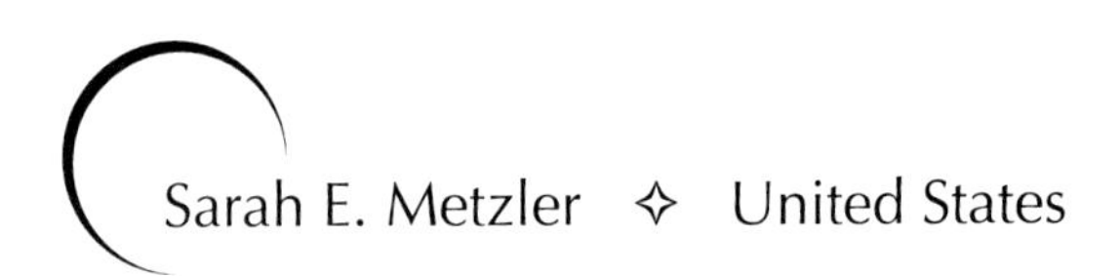

Sarah E. Metzler ✧ United States

the lone star state of her pregnancy

Mark Miller ✧ Australia

wildlife sign —
pinpoints of light through
the bullet holes

Mircea Moldovan ✧ Romania

autumn haze
father begs me
to take him home

Beverly Acuff Momoi ✧ United States

winter dusk settling on the beneficiaries

winter stars
the distant places
we keep our grief

Joanne Morcom ✧ Canada

assisted living funeral home calendars

Laurie D. Morrissey ✧ United States

old storybook—
Dad's accent
on every page

Daipayan Nair ✧ India

buzzing flies —
men discuss politics
in a tea stall

John Newson ✧ United Kingdom

grieving
the last piece of cake
at the funeral

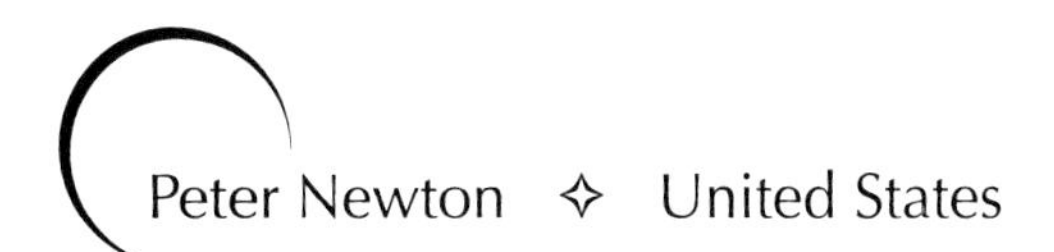

Peter Newton ✧ United States

museum bone flute
the original owner
a bird

Subir Ningthouja ✧ India

the space between stars —
a missing child
remains missing

Réka Nyitrai ✧ Romania

the moon a woman mending my husband's socks

William O'Sullivan ✧ United States

lilies of the valley . . .
giving prayer
one more try

church play
halo and wings
on the bully

funeral procession
the sounds
silent people make

Rita Odeh ✧ Israel

setting sun —
the field silenced
crow by crow

Debbie Olson ✧ United States

she nibbles the tip
of his ear
chocolate rabbit

Roland Packer ✧ Canada

foyer portraits . . .
the old headmasters'
stink eye

Tom Painting ✧ United States

nothing settled
a gust of wind rattles
the chimney flue

patchwork quilt
    I silently slip out of
my married name

custody battle
the uneven breaking
of a wishbone

Jacquie Pearce ✧ Canada

curtain of rain
holding off the moment
we part

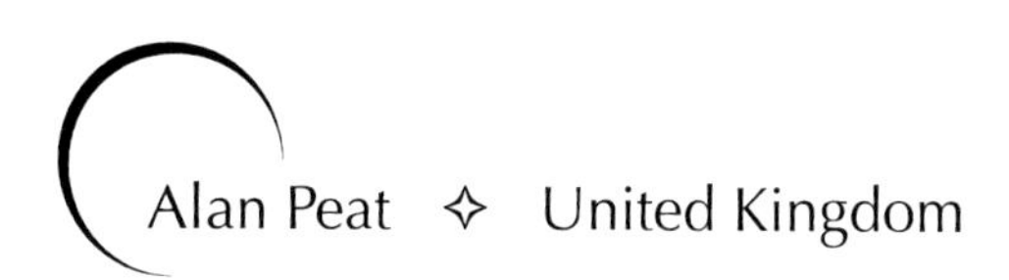

Alan Peat ✧ United Kingdom

snow buries everything
behind the calendar
we gave them

Pippa Phillips ✧ United States

early sunset —
the blue disappearing
from my mother's eyes

Gregory Piko ✧ Australia

cooking for one
she leaves the door
ajar

Sanela Pliško ✧ Croatia

lonely evening
I give a name to
a wine fly

Ruth Powell ✧ Canada

just the nose
of a meadow vole
deep winter

Thomas Powell ✧ Northern Ireland/Wales

summer dusk . . .
talking to a farmer
I take the fox's side

Sandi Pray ✧ United States

what you said
in last night's dream
morning tea

spring morning
the postie stops to give
my dog a treat

autumn winds . . .
my dead neighbor's pickup
fills with leaves

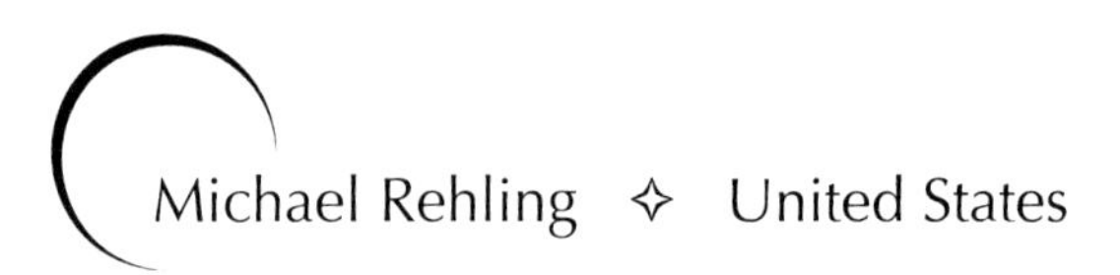

Michael Rehling ✧ United States

two boats
at the dock
touching   not touching

Sharon Rhutasel-Jones ✧ United States

church steeple
its dark shadows
on the park swings

Bryan Rickert ✧ United States

all the cats
in one window
morning birdsong

Edward J. Rielly ✧ United States

reading obituaries
my wife and I
side by side

Chad Lee Robinson ✧ United States

small town diner —
in three crayons or less
the prairie landscape

Ashley Rodman ✧ United States

distant thunder
the underlined words
in my library book

Michele Root-Bernstein ✧ United States

spring morning
a little i
in everything

Jacob D. Salzer ✧ United States

finally
without a business suit
summer wind

Srinivasa Rao Sambangi ✧ India

online dating
she asks if I can
brighten the screen

Agnes Eva Savich ✧ United States

my father says
around the next bend
the chill autumn air

Rich Schilling ✧ United States

blazing sun
my wife watering
the kids

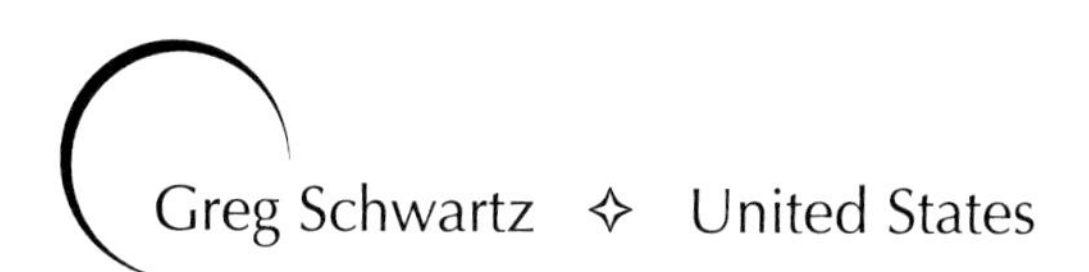

Greg Schwartz ✧ United States

anniversary sex
the light
still on

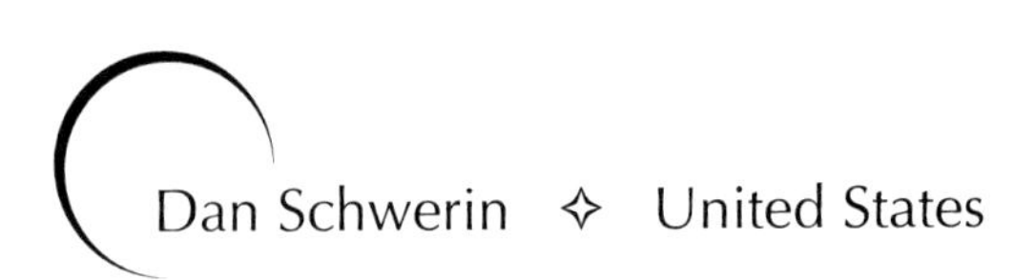

we can't say schizophrenia rain in the funeral tent

metal roof
how the rain wants
to be remembered

if she floats, America

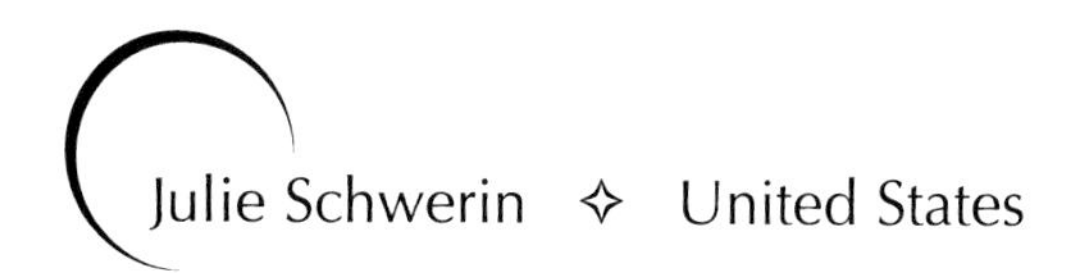

Julie Schwerin ✧ United States

Easter morning
hyacinths push
the stones aside

left behind
in the move
the bowl
all the other bowls
fit inside

carrying on
without me . . .
the bluebells

sekiro ✧ United States

buddha belly—
all that's left
of my buddhism

Maureen Sexton ✧ Australia

my mother asks
if I am her sister . . .
entry to the maze

Adelaide B. Shaw ✧ United States

trick or treat
waiting for the grandchildren
of strangers

Nancy Shires ✧ United States

obituary
icing covering
cracks in the cake

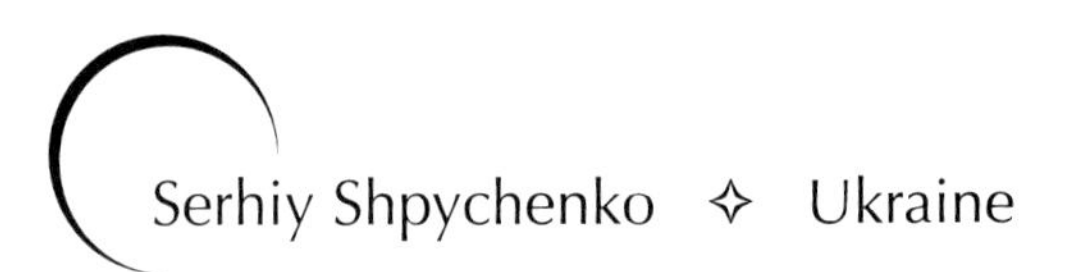
Serhiy Shpychenko ✧ Ukraine

quarantined city . . .
equal distance between trees
on the boulevard

Sandra Simpson ✧ New Zealand

a blizzard of petals —
we all laugh
in the same language

Neena Singh ✧ India

dragonfly—
the friend who went
without a goodbye

Laszlo Slomovits ✧ United States

sparks from the campfire
the little lies
that improve the story

Robin Smith ✧ United States

Queen Anne's lace
in the bridal bouquet
her wild streak

Mary Stevens ✧ United States

the retirement plan
wants my permanent address
summer clouds

John Stevenson ✧ United States

an honorable mention
in the death poem
contest

Barbara Strang ✧ New Zealand

lockdown
across the lake a traffic light
switches to green

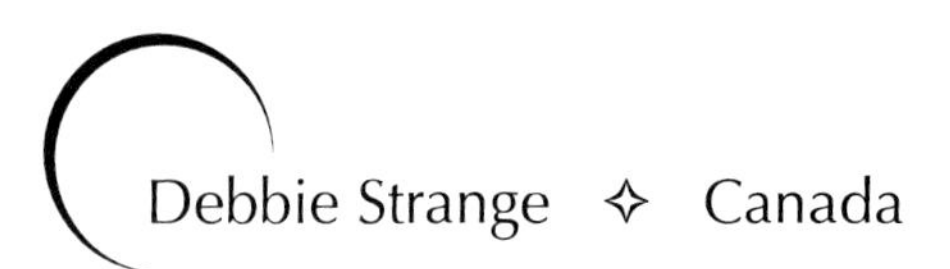

Debbie Strange ✧ Canada

estuary light
the treble clefs
of flamingos

Alan Summers ✧ United Kingdom

Easter Monday
a couple try to jump
the ticket barrier

Nathanael Tico ✧ United States

mansplaining
mansplaining

Stephen Toft ✧ United Kingdom

blue sky
the pause before
the swing returns

bedridden
waltzing
with her hands

bedtime
my son asks me how far it is
to the war

after the funeral
the sound wind makes
in tall grasses

family gathering —
the slow tick
of the grandfather clock

Michael Dylan Welch ✧ United States

heirloom bowl—
a few granny smiths
beginning to wrinkle

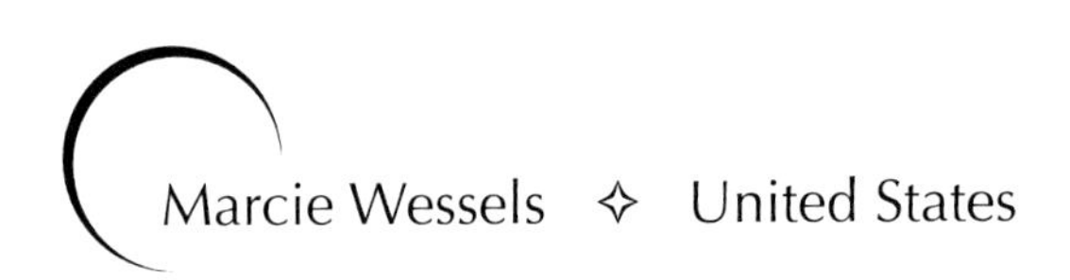

Marcie Wessels ✧ United States

ash-throated flycatcher the pale-yellow hitch in its song

Ian Willey ✧ Japan

French word for snow on the tip of my tongue

Tony Williams ✧ United Kingdom

morning news . . .
I scrape the darkness
from my toast

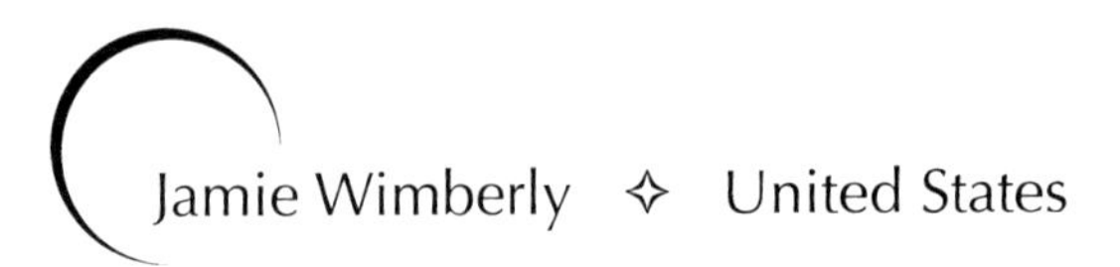

Jamie Wimberly ✧ United States

a gesture
is all —
white tulip

sheila windsor ✧ United Kingdom

child's grave
the plastic windmill
still still

Robert Witmer ✧ Japan

a silent nightingale in her throat cancer

Genevieve Wynand ✧ Canada

considering
the first draft
spring garden

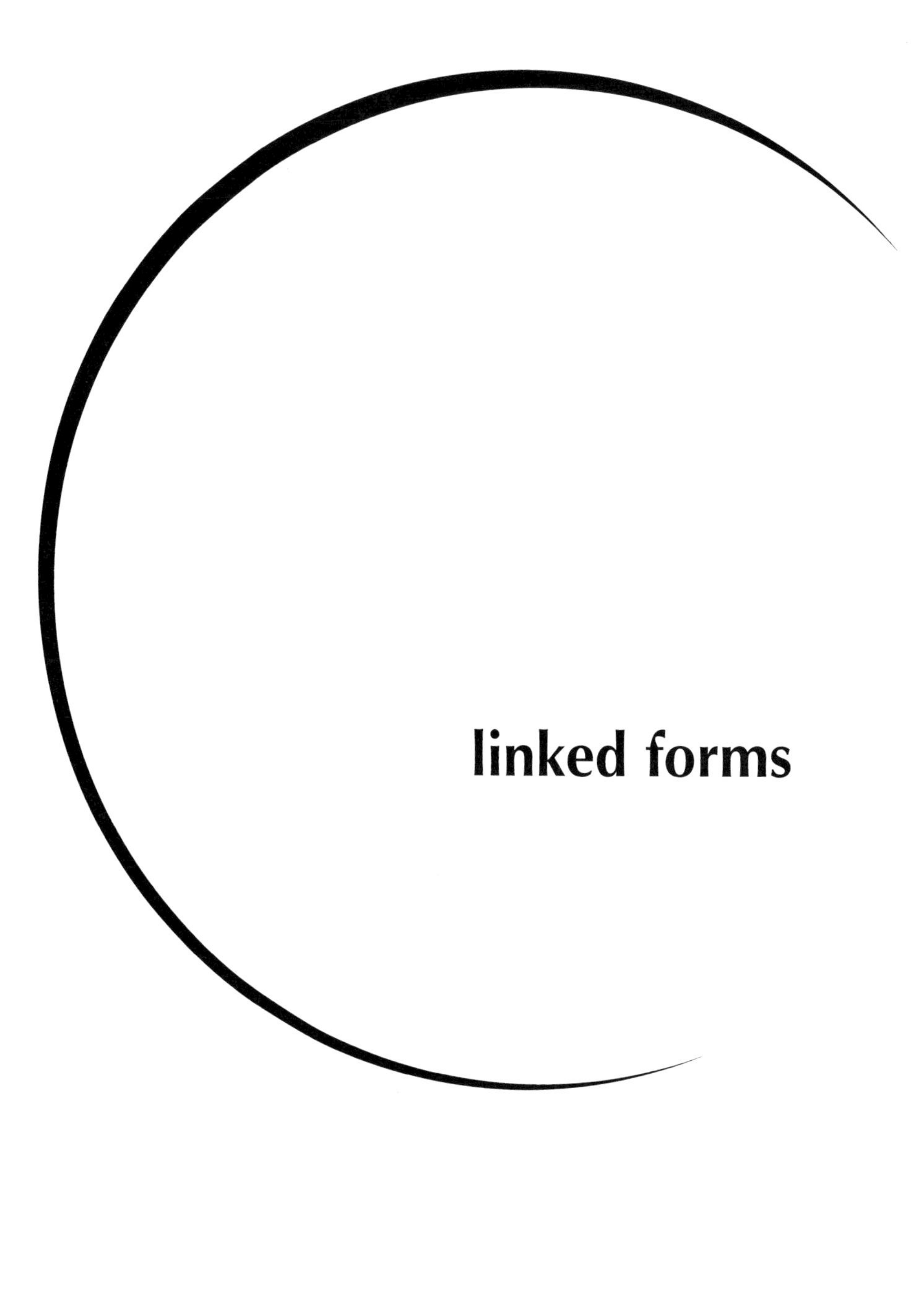

linked forms

Inheritance

She never eats at the table. If she can't drink it or eat it while headed out the door, she leaves it alone.

morning
the long commute
from hand to mouth

The cherry farmhouse table is where all the fighting started. The one piece of furniture everyone else wanted after Mother died.

first AA meeting
she takes the seat
her mother left her

Roberta Beary ✧ United States/Ireland

What the Magdalen Asylum Scrubbed Clean

buttonhole daisy
losing itself
petal by petal

The church bells are a ringing reproach. I missed early mass with Mother, and go alone to take communion. Father is a man to be trusted. So when he beckons, I follow into the back room. Empty after the altar boys have dispersed.

deep inside
the silver chalice
a taste of honey

That night Mother kneels me before the Sacred Heart. She will call me a disgrace for the rest of our Sundays together. Until she takes me to the place where I separate lights from darks. And count my days into before and after.

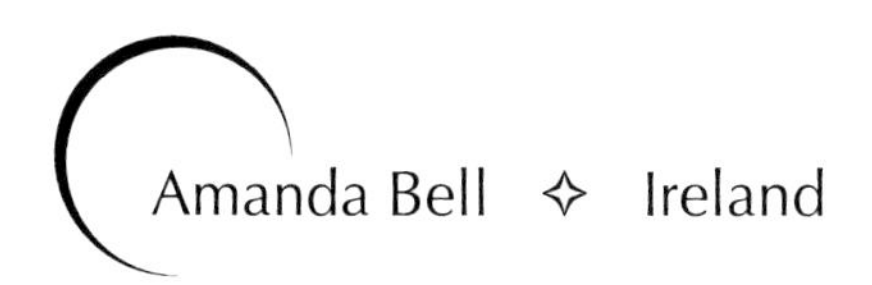
Amanda Bell ✧ Ireland

Glass Half-Full

Each time a ceiling collapsed, they shrugged it off and moved into the next room, and the next again. What I remember most though is the warmth of the kitchen, the glow of humanity in fluorescent light, and a cat who slept on top of the grill, with his tail sweeping down to the hob. They made their own wine, and stored it in demijohns under the table, syphoning it straight into glasses through a rubber tube. I remember how in love they were. She must have been the age that I am now, and nothing bad had happened yet, nothing really bad.

after the service
in trusses of ivy flowers
slow-drifting wasps

(Un)growing Up

Pushing a finger into the dry soil of the overwintered pot, I look up and catch sight of a school bus full of heads barely making it into their window view. One face in each window, each half covered in a sky-blue mask, head cuddled in hoodie, only a bit of eyes and forehead. I realize it's the first time in years I've seen a bus full of such young ones. It all comes into focus, how things are. The separateness, the changes. Is it easier or harder now for those children? Not talking to someone, no one scrunched in beside them, the laughter and words of others silenced. Just staring through their bit of glass out into the cold, watching the morning take root. I remember my own bus rides and how there were times I needed others around me, the sounds, the encapsulated chaos. And the times I prayed for separateness to feel safe. I guess either scenario could stunt a person, depending.

tender bulb
trying to force it
before its time

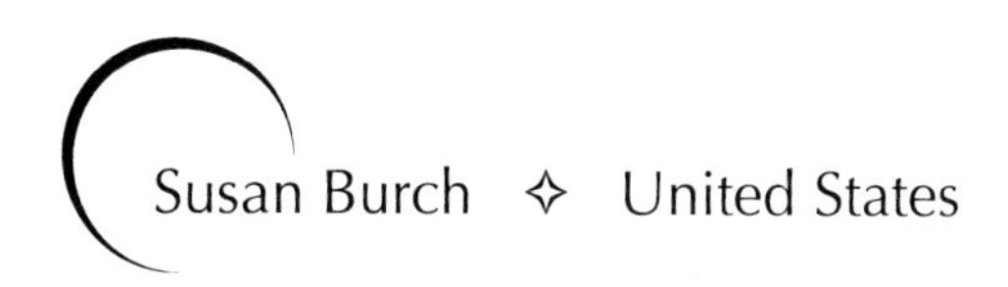

Susan Burch ✧ United States

My Husband Laughs at Me, but . . .

sometimes eating raisin bran feels like too much work. The bran is crunchy & the raisins are chewy & it's so much effort in every bite.

JAWS how did he do it

Pris Campbell ✧ United States

Casting Couch

My old college chaplain, now working in Manhattan, meets me there during an APA meeting. We've kept in touch by mail over the years. "Big H", he calls himself, his name reflecting his height and girth, the way he carries himself confidently through crowds. His hair grown shoulder length, hippie style, he spots me right away at my hotel lobby, sweeping me up for a giant hug, letting the circling men know I've been claimed. We have lunch at a nearby, overpriced deli, talking nonstop. Late twenties now, I still tell him all my secrets, my breakdown over a friend's suicide, fiancé headed to Vietnam at the same time. He says he's into orgies and has an open marriage. If he's trying to shock me he doesn't succeed.

When he walks me back to my room he comes inside. Soon he's telling me he wants out of the mentor role; he wants an "adult" relationship with me. I agree that would be a good change. He adds that means having sex. I tell him I DON'T agree with that part. He tells me if I don't do it he'll assume I just want to lean on him and that will be the end of our relationship.

I'm torn up inside. I don't want to lose him. He's been my knight in shining armor, the man on the white horse. He pushes even harder to convince me, moving closer, hands hard on my shoulders.

The walls of the room close in. My heart pounds. I feel like an animal in a cage. I'm furious but feel the fight in me ebbing. Finally, I lean back on the bed. "If it's so important, just do it," I snap, certain the man I thought he was will draw back and apologize but he shoves into me, his face rough against mine. My body is frozen. I've become a hole. Who can ever understand how strong a muzzle power is? He's my secret rape. When he's done, he smiles, pulls on his jeans, and leaves without a word.

bitter rain
a lost dog cries
in the night

The Green Zone

No new cases for the past twenty-one days. For the first time in his life, dad has stopped shaving. The beard suits him. But he doesn't look in the mirror. He has also stopped wearing his watch. He looks out the window. A lot. He walks the street with his eyes. Then he walks the skies. He's happy when there are some clouds to walk along with. He eats his dinner quietly. Almost. Twice during the meal, he says the word, Covid. He washes his plate and goes to the window. He's jumping from star to star.

little moth
crosses the street
wind on my face

Nightfall

Just as I do every day, I sit by his bed and unwrap one of the snacks I packed for myself in the morning. As I crunch into a cracker, this man who has always seen me as much more special than I am, becomes agitated. His hand waves butterfly-like, as he asks me to go eat at one of the benches outside. Sad looks flash across both of our faces. He tells me the noise is too much to bear.

hospital bed
watching the sun
begin its descent

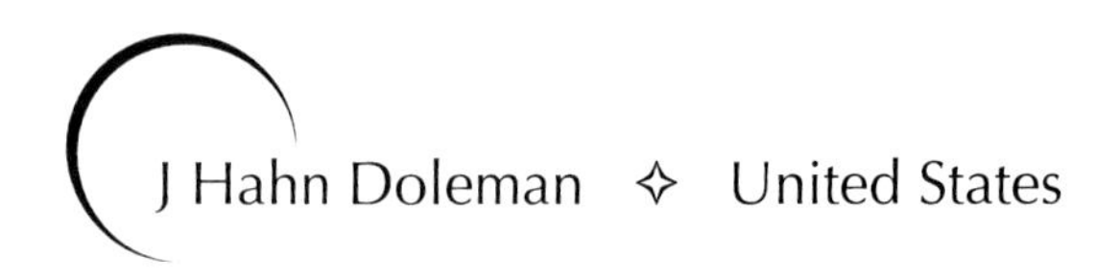

The Right Way

Granddad tells my parents they ought to think about fixing me sooner than later. There are whispers of something sinister. He advises several remedies, such as rapping my knuckles with a wooden ruler. My father demurs, but not entirely, buying me a first baseman's mitt aligned with my way of looking at the world. But standing me on the awkward side of home plate when it's my turn at bat. The upshot being although I strike out more times than not, I'm a reliable defensive player.

junco nest
the stunted fledgling
left behind

When Candy Bars Were a Nickel

The way a sneeze comes on, my younger sister can't stop herself. It is all about the candy bar. She slides over the front seat and leans on the door handle to thrust her hand in the grocery bag.

I am six years old, in the back seat looking at dad's head. I say nothing. It's a frozen silence I drift in. At first he doesn't hear the wind gush or the scream of knowing, until some awareness grabs him.

The car comes to a screeching halt. He is wearing a cap and baggy overalls. He is running frantic right and left back along the country road. He is a scarecrow flapping. He is a stalk of corn walking. He is a spray of wheat undulating. He is an oat seed. He is invisible.

sidestepping roots
in the woodland
he won't talk about it

Terri L. French ✧ United States

The Red Sweater

It's the holiday season. I'm wandering around the mall in a daze. The music is too loud, the lights too bright, the displays festively garish. And the people. In and out of the stores ladened with shopping bags, up and down the escalators, standing in line to plop squalling children onto Santa's lap. I go into one department store and head to the clearance rack. A red sweater catches my eye. It's 10-percent off the already discounted price. I buy it without trying it on and quickly make my way to the parking lot. Fresh, cold air hits my face, wakes me up to why I was here in the first place. Just to get away. Just to be in the midst of the sensory overload of Christmas. I didn't want to think about what my son had told me over the phone this morning. That his best friend had died from an overdose in his kitchen as he'd sat on the floor holding him. Later I'll try on this red sweater, seeing in the mirror the look on my face that says "It could have been him."

child's birthday party
one boy huffing
helium balloons

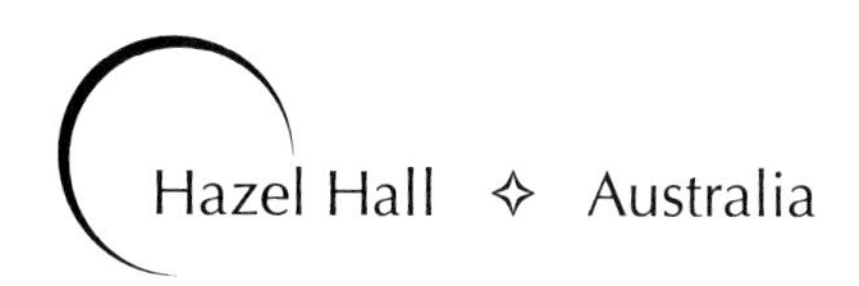

Into the Light

The woman in the blue dressing gown, long white hair, long white socks and fluffy red slippers, is drifting around the nursing home. She's searching through the rooms for something lost. A large black shoulder bag is hung across her body as if she is about to board a bus. Each time she wanders to the entrance lobby and tries the automatic doors, they will not open. A member of the receptionist staff takes her gently by the elbow saying Elaine, it's time to rest. He leads her back through the long corridor until they both disappear into the peaceful order again. One day she will find what she is seeking. A receptionist will take her gently by the elbow saying Elaine, it's time to go. Then the staff will form a guard of honour. The automatic doors will open to a sky as blue as her dressing gown. A bright red bus will be waiting outside. The driver will take her elbow saying Watch your step, Elaine. She will board without a ticket and the bus will lift into the clean, fresh air and disappear within clouds softer than her long white hair.

rush of wind —
swallows carry
the autumn away

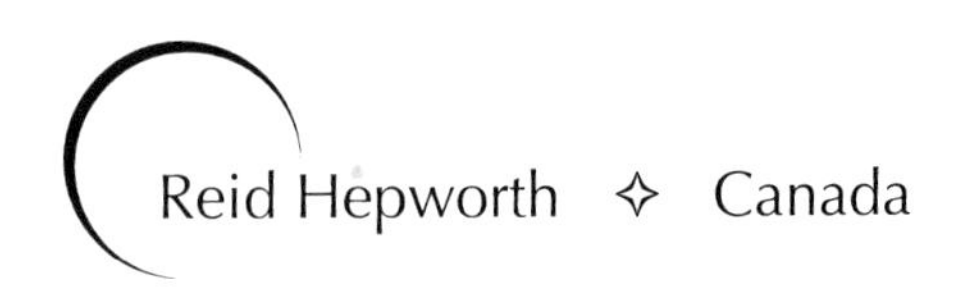

Reid Hepworth ✧ Canada

Chance Meeting

The animal waddles onto the road. My mind registers that it's a dog as I drive past. "What the heck", I think as I double-check my rear-view mirror and scramble to find a place to pull over.

The dog, a rotund little dachshund with a pink bejewelled collar, noses around the edge of the highway as I play death-wish running in and out of traffic.

My nerves are shot by the time I reach the dog. Sensing me and the busy roadway, the dog stops sniffing and stares at me with its orb-like eyes. Its pintsized head is a study in still life. It looks like it's willing itself to disappear.

I hear the squeal of brakes before I see the semi-truck. I quickly grab the dog and pick it up. Not an easy feat with twenty-five pounds of dead weight and a bad back.

date night we laugh about how we met

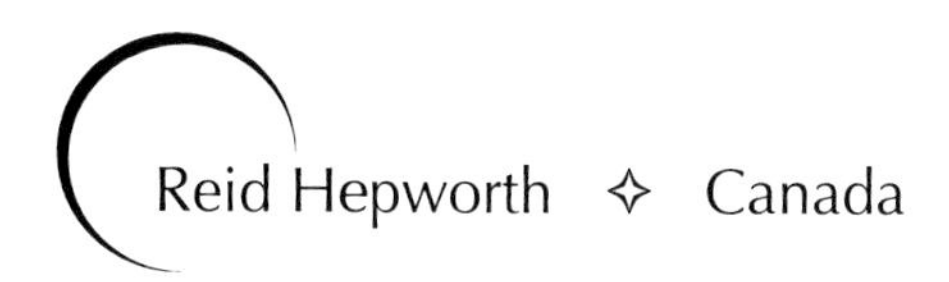

Fresh Start

Grade 3. Skinned knees and a pixie cut. Mum's last attempt to keep me in pigtails and dresses has failed. I've set my limits and have started picking out my own clothes. No more waking up and seeing skirt-sets laid out at the bottom of my bed.

the thinnest sliver

Mum quietly cringes at my fashion choices; dad calls me his "little bra burner" when I refuse to wear my bikini top at the beach. I am secretly pleased when a total stranger mistakes me for a boy.

of light through the trees

I want to fit in as much as everyone does, but my friends have long hair, wear mood rings and listen to pop rock. I listen to Gloria Steinem on TV with the growing realization that times are changing. Just not quickly enough.

new moon

I make my stand at dinner. I refuse to clean the dishes while the men sit at the dining table talking politics. My dad grins as he picks up his plate.

Van Gogh's Ear

A drunken evening, both men soused and twitchy. An argument ensues with Yellow House roommate Paul Gauguin. The two dissing each other's work like clicking beetles. Seething, Vincent picks up a threatening straight razor. Gauguin edges away as Vincent turns the razor on himself, cutting off his left ear in a rage. The appendage falls to the floor, where Vincent's dog Angelus snatches the bloody ear snidling back under the nearby bed, where she'd been cowering during the set-to.

grey air —
shivering
in my lungs

Angelus chews on the fallen treat. Vincent, bleeding profusely and cursing the dog, drops to his knees stretching an arm under the bed. Gauguin sobered by the mayhem drops to his knees to help retrieve the ear from Angelus' jaws. Dust bunnies fly from their efforts. A whacking broom frees the masticated ear, scooting from under the bed like a lost toy.

Towel pressed against his wound Vincent picks up the ear, wrapping it in a half-sheet of newspaper. *Now what?* shouts Gauguin. Van Gogh rushes out the door to the Arles brothel where earlier he and Gauguin were hard drinking and falling out over Rachel, a favorite of the two. The young woman's aghast to receive the grotesque gift, stained by newsprint ink.

night stars
striking
through mist

Wanly smiling, a blood-soaked Van Gogh returns home, collapsing unconscious on his bed. The next morning attracted by Angelus' howling, police are called. Vincent's taken to the hospital by a local gendarme—Rachel sends along the ear. The artist is near death. Fearing implication Gauguin hastily returns to Paris by train.

Van Gogh survives his injury. A week later back home he paints two self-portraits showing a thickly bandaged right ear: mirror images. Vincent never speaks of the incident. A Dr. Ray may have kept the dog-mangled ear, taken the token home to his own dog. All the facts are disputed. There are, of course, the two self-portraits. An earlier painting called *Dog* presents a medium size dog opened-jaw, snarling, about to leap . . .

sunflowers
brash yellow
fill the field

Manzanar War Relocation Center

between orders
the sound of wind chimes
from metal forks

rich or poor
same desert
for a garden

desert wind
the sound of jump ropes
double Dutch

a long home run
off the guard tower
first to clap, the guard

past the guard tower
a Sunday family stroll
without looking up

family portrait
a kid in the army cap
of big brother

from the radio
the emperor's surrender
our posture perfect

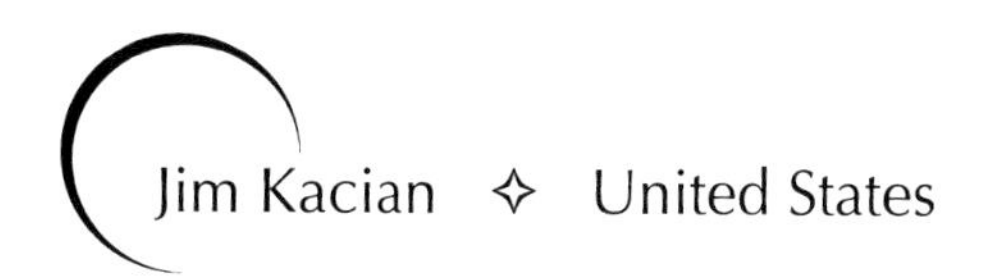

Jim Kacian ✧ United States

every night

we fall down a hole where all the other animals live, sometimes deep, sometimes not

what's down there doesn't need any explanation

every morning we climb out and try to make sense of it anyway

what's special about us is that we think we can, and can pass it along to others

in a tent in the rain i become a climate

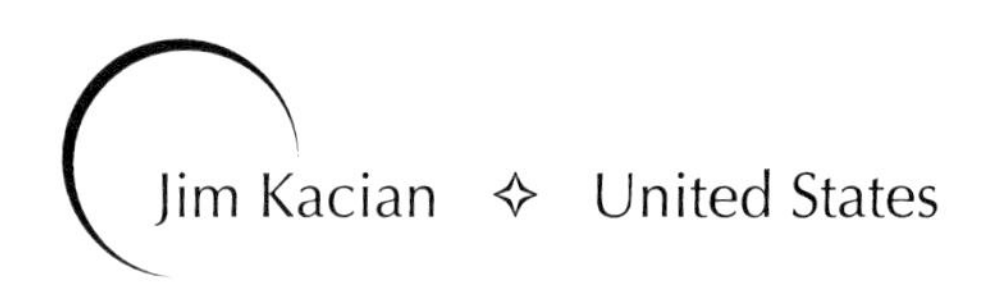

The Colonies

We have been right from the beginning. but in the wrong way. The gods did come from the heavens, but they were not more glorious versions of ourselves. They were the microbes hitchhiking through space on comets that crashed our planet some 3 billion years ago. One-celled organisms that could withstand the cold and the dark and the vacuum of space, the lack of oxygen, the radiation, the loneliness in a billion miles. Monocytes landed here, found a habitable planet, and began their colonization, until today they reign supreme. Unassailable in their simplicity, they have permitted a small series of permutations endlessly reiterated to arise into what seems like complexity to insufficient brains. They have permitted consciousness to come into being, and with it belief systems and ambitions far removed from their own interests. For in truth we are merely the transport vehicles for these gods, a means of migration, hosts, and we carry a cloud of them before us everywhere we go, and leave a trail of them wherever we have been. Even our awareness of their hegemony cannot matter to them, since they are more alien, more adaptable, more ubiquitous than we can ever be. They have permitted us to see them only as isolated, if teeming, colonies, but if we could hold them at a remove, consider them all at the same time, we would see them as they really are: the chaotic, teeming, ineluctable face of God.

microwave static
from light years
and others

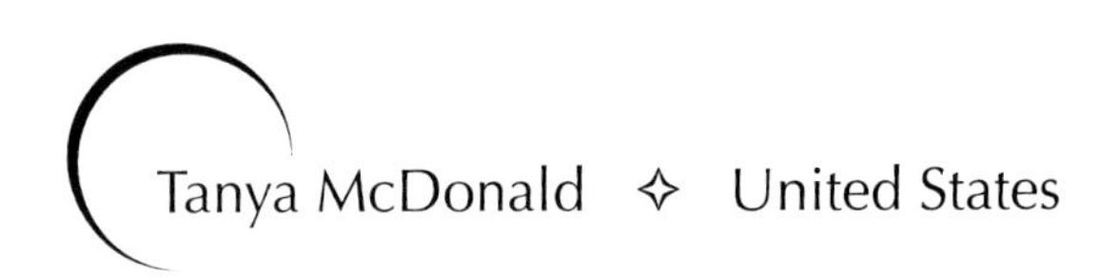

Tanya McDonald ✧ United States

Take Me Out

evening ballgame
behind the Stars & Stripes
a Pride flag

Crackerjacks —
the prize
of feeling ten again

second strike —
high above the infield
a tern changes course

bases loaded —
a steady stream
of inbound planes

chat on the mound . . .
the fan cam
catches a kiss

seventh inning stretch
the long whistle
of a freight train

Sean O'Connor ✧ Ireland

Perfection

Just days old, the four babies lie crossways in a single cot. Four round faces; mouths gasping, their unfocused eyes swimming with wonder.

A blanket has been clipped above the cot to protect them from flying glass should the windows blow in.

> Spring sunlight —
> so perfectly formed
> eight tiny hands

Alan Peat ✧ United Kingdom

last orders

I have, of late, been thinking of all the places that we didn't see together; of things I wish you'd lived to see. There are, of course, mountains, sprinkled with little lakes, so clear you'd have laughed as minnows swam freely through your body's reflection. There are coastal paths; forest walks; curlews in flight; a dolphin chaperoning our boat; a pure green field of playful lambs. And there are also tall-ceilinged rooms in stately homes, so stuffed with bone china and twist-stemmed glass that you'd have stopped in your tracks and shaken your head as you took it all in. I can see that look on your face quite clearly.

half moon
my hand-pulled pint just the way
you'd have liked it

Letter From Basho to Robert Frost

Here too, my old friend, the woods are white with winter, their branches spread against the sky like omikuji papers which bring tidings of fortune, both good and bad. Leaves long lost to wind and weather now lie buried like brush marks which I have not yet been able to cajole into calligraphy. A faint sun lingers overhead like the echo of a far-off temple bell, and ice spreads over the pond like a Noh player's mask.

> origami days
> a red-crowned crane
> unfolding in flight

Listen: do you hear the forest speaking through the hollow of the owl, the saw-sound of the raven, the rasp of the wren? By hearth's light, I put ink to paper the way a koi swirls before surfacing, just as I imagine the movement of your pen spreading apple-roots across the page. At the foot of the mountain, in my small hut, I turn my face to the moon, white as a chrysanthemum, and wonder what poem you are dreaming of tonight in your woods so dark and deep. Across these centuries, in this one world, and at this quiet hour, I send you this letter to wish you well and to say that I, too, often stop on my way home to hear horse bells jingling in the cold.

fallen blossoms . . .
where distant neighbors meet
to mend the wall

Keith Polette ✧ United States

Gossip

When I was a boy, my great-grandmother, who once had a job playing the piano accompaniment to silent movies, told me that trees like to gossip, especially in autumn. The elms, she said, liked to whisper behind the backs of sugar maples, smirking that no respectable tree should flash so much red. And the sugar maples, staying silent as window store mannequins, would wait for a hard wind so they could flash the underside of their scarlet leaves to the elms, who would quickly yellow and turn away.

> ruby red sunset
> the smudge of lipstick
> on a shirt collar

Given their few numbers, shagbark hickory trees, their bark thrusting out like shingles curling on the roof of an old farmhouse, are spoken about with pity by the other trees, the way one might talk about a three-legged dog or an old man with psoriasis.

winter shed
stiff empty work gloves
clutching nothing

But the tree that is most disdained and the subject of the harshest talk is the pin oak, not only because of its helmet-hard bark but because it holds onto its leaves deep into winter, while the rest of the trees, bare and bald, shiver with resentment.

rusted lock
refusing to release the key . . .
dead of winter

Bryan Rickert ✧ United States
Kat Lehmann ✧ United States

The Next Day

departing autumn
a day moon divided
by contrails

first chill
this night alone

daybreak
the simplicity
of one plate

winding yarn
hours of chit-chat
with the cat

filling the silence
a tea pot's whistle

last sip . . .
to toss or to mend
this chipped cup

Aberfan

1961 garbled words from space my father back from the pub

1962 click of a stopwatch again last under the desk

1963 nicking a Beano from the newsstand JFK dead

1964 Beatles land in New York creeping downstairs

1965 early hours a phantom punch in the first round

1966 Rumours throughout the school. Older boys picked up at the gates by fathers. Classes cancelled. Walking home through silent streets. Our front door ajar. A note from Dad that he's gone to help, back in a couple of days. Grabbing an apple. Cycling past the biscuit factory, into Roath, then Llanishen, heading for Merthyr. A puncture in the dark. A chill in the air. A police car taking me home. The helplessness. The fear. The dark.

surfacing my body picked clean by crows

Clocking Out from the Crab Factory

And me cocksure waiting at the gates. She cracks a tired smile, slides one chafed hand into mine. The other holds a weighted plastic bag. She is much older, and intoxicating. Her hair smells of the ocean. Two minutes later we are on the harbor's seawall, our legs dangling over granite. Scallops too small to make the cut laid out between us. She opens one, touches its muscular foot with her knife, watches it react and withdraw. "That's what they all do," she says, before biting into the meat.

finding the grave
by her given name
wild flowers

Endings

He never spoke about the time he served in Vietnam. The only thing I know for certain is when he came back, he changed his name.

autumn wind
a cloud drifts
apart

Quiet Corner

As a child, I attended a village school where the playground shared a wall with the churchyard. On one side of the wall, we played and shouted. On the other, a line of small mossy memorials marked the graves of babies. Having grown up knowing that I had a sister who had died before I was born, I accepted, as did most people, that babies died. Years later, staring in wonder at my firstborn, I would think about those stones again, the tiny bodies that they covered, and from a new perspective, the parents.

snail shells
the song thrush uses gravestones
for an anvil

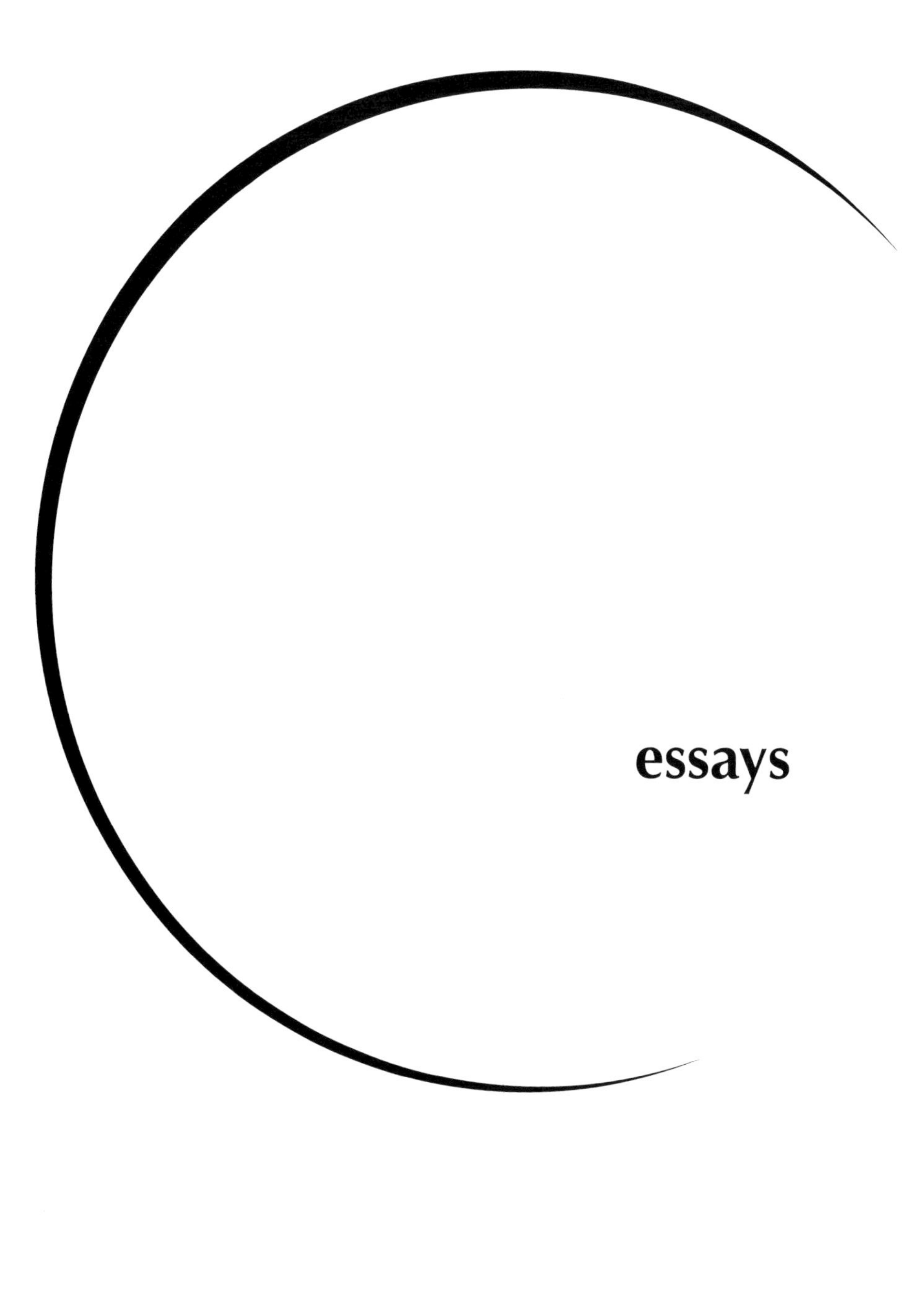

essays

Akito Arima ♦ Japan

"Haiku" to Contribute to World Peace

On July 22, 2016, a promoters' council was born for the mission of having "haiku" registered on the List of UNESCO World Intangible Cultural Heritage.

Jointly with Sakae Okamoto, Mayor of Iga City, Mie Prefecture (the well-known city as Matsuo Bashō's birth place), I, as President of Haiku International Association (HIA), had appealed for the necessity of the launch meeting of the Promoters Council. Enthusiastically gathered together for the launching meeting were representatives of the 3 major Japanese haiku associations: Association of Haiku Poets (President: Shugyo Takaha), Modern Haiku Association (President: Shizuo Miyasaka) and Association of Japanese Classical Haiku (President: Teiko Inahata). Another member of the Council, Koji Kawamoto, Emeritus Professor at the University of Tokyo, was unfortunately unable to attend.

In the immediate future, we intend to start up a task force for progressing the UNESCO Plan by inviting those people from municipal corporations and bodies which are related to Bashō and other traditional haiku masters. We will also invite individual haiku lovers who belong to the three major haiku associations and HIA for joining the task force team.

As you all know, haiku, perhaps the shortest poetry in the world, is an art of Japanese literature with its proud history. Haiku has been gaining popularity in many countries, as well as in Japan. It is no exaggeration to say that haiku provides people with a "reason for living." Men and women, from children to adults up to the great age of one hundred and over, are enjoying making and reading haiku.

Haiku was introduced overseas more than a hundred years ago. In 2015, in his welcoming speech for Mr. Herman Van Rompuy, the first President of the European Council whom HIA invited as the guest speaker of our annual convention, Ambassador Viorel Isticioaia-Budura of the EU Delegation to Japan shared the fact that Hendrik Doeff, Chief of the Dutch trading settlements on Dejima in Nagasaki, was the first Westerner who is known to have written haiku.

In 1983, President Ronald W. Reagan of the United States delivered a speech in a session of Japan's House of Representatives. He quoted Matsuo Bashō's haiku:

> Many kinds of plants
> And each one triumphant in its special blossoms
> *(Translation inscribed on the memorial tablet located in Iga City)*

In 2013 in Washington, Caroline B. Kennedy, U.S. Ambassador to Japan, quoted one sentence from the beginning part of the prose and haiku, *The Narrow Road to the Deep North*, by Matsuo Bashō, just before leaving for her new appointment."The guardian spirits of the road beckoned, and I could not settle down to work." She meant she couldn't wait to get to work in Japan. The aforementioned Mr. Van Rompuy, the former President of the EU, who has published two haiku anthologies already, said that his most favorite haiku master is Bashō. During his short stay in Japan, Mr. Van Rompuy visited Karuizawa, Nagano Prefecture where he saw the stone tablet on which Bashō's haiku was engraved:

snowy morning so fine
that I take a close look
even at the familiar horse

(tr. Toru Kiuchi)

All in all, I want to emphasize the importance of the location where the launch meeting of the Council for the "Haiku for UNESCO" took place — "Iga City" where Matsuo Bashō, the greatest haiku master of worldwide fame, was born.

Bashō was born in 1644 in the province of Iga (present Iga City). In his teens, he learned haiku from Kitamura Kigin who lived in Kyoto. Iga Province was rather close to Kyoto (then Japan's capital). At the age of 29, Bashō decided to head for Edo (present Tokyo) where he hoped to vitalize his haiku career and to usher in a new phase into haiku circles. Edo in those days was far behind Kyoto in a sense of haiku's development. In his last 20 or so years until he died at 51 in Osaka, Bashō showed an outstanding artistic talent in the haiku world. And the blossoms of his haiku were passed on to the next generation by his followers such as Kawai Sora, Takarai Kikaku and Mukai Kyorai.

What follows are the main topics of the heated discussions during the "promoters' launch meeting". As a result, we all agreed that attractive aspects of haiku should be all the more widely known.

Mass Appeal of Haiku: Mainly because of its simplicity, people around the world, irrespective of age and sex, can enjoy creating haiku. As evidence, entrants for the recent HIA's Haiku Contest represented as many as 49 countries.

Universality of Haiku: Allen Ginsberg, an American poet wrote many short poems like haiku, also using nature as its theme. Facts have it in addition that two distinguished Swedes both wrote haiku — Thomas Tranströmer, the poet of national pride (the Nobel laureate in literature), and the late Dag Hammarskjöld, former Secretary-General of the United Nations (who received the Nobel Peace Prize after his death).

Those facts — even top-class poets and great politicians create haiku — show how universal haiku is in principle. On the other hand, people on the street have discovered and begun to enjoy haiku-writing mainly because of its simplicity, resulting in a remarkable increase of poets all over the world.

Peace and Haiku: Subjects of haiku come from observation of nature and daily living. Haiku can change a moment into eternity. Observation of nature leads to the spirit of nature conservation, mutual understanding of people and ultimately to "world peace."

Transcending Education for the Next Generation: To enhance one's sensibility for usage of words increases self-expression capability and trains the mind to extract one's thoughts succinctly. We understand that some of the primary schools in the United States are employing haiku in class to nurture children's creative expression.

Hopefully, if haiku is registered on the UNESCO List, language ability of Japanese children, as well as of children around the world, will certainly be improved.

Through haiku, we, haiku lovers, are connected each other worldwide. As an example, In 2016 HIA invited a lecturer from Vietnam to speak at its Annual Lecture Meeting. The lecturer was Ms. Nguyen Vu Quynh Nhu, Visiting Research Scholar of International Research Center for Japanese Studies in Kyoto, Japan. Ms. Nhu obtained a doctoral degree on literature (for haiku studies) from Ho Chi Minh University of Social Sciences and Humanities. Her encounter with haiku was through our house bulletin *HI*, every issue of which is being delivered to embassies and legations abroad through the Ministry of Foreign Affairs. She is now teaching haiku to the Vietnamese people. The case of Ms. Nhu is an example of universality in haiku poetry I mentioned above. Let me repeat that haiku is spreading worldwide, as well as in Japan, because of its advantage of being a short form of poetry. Another advantage is the distinct features in which subjects of haiku writing are mainly on the blessings of nature or on harmonious coexistence between human lives and nature.

I'm more than pleased to say that a movement to have "Haiku" registered as one of the UNESCO intangible cultural treasures around the world is under way. thanks to the joint forces of haiku-related municipalities such as Iga City and four major haiku associations in Japan including HIA.

My fellow HIA members, your cooperation and joint efforts are sincerely requested.

(Translation into English by Shoji Matsumoto.)

Brad Bennett ✧ United States

Euphony in Haiku

"The sound must seem an echo to the sense."
Alexander Pope[1]

The sensory haiku moment, whether experienced or created in the poem itself, is crucial to a successful haiku. It's always been the main focus for me. But the haiku is, of course, a poem, and poems are designed to be read aloud. When we listen to a poem, we are attracted to its pleasing sounds and how they create unity in the poem. A successful haiku resonates. It coheres. So, as haiku poets, we need to think about how our poems sound, in addition to whether we've captured the haiku moment. If we are able to construct an authentic haiku moment, and also choose words made of sounds that enhance the music, create more unity, and add to the meaning or emotional resonance of the poem, then we are getting the most out of our poems.

I was inspired to dive more deeply into this examination of euphony by two experts in the use of this technique.

1. Pope, Alexander. "An Essay on Criticism: Part 2." From www.poetryfoundation.org/poems/44897/an-essay-on-criticism-part-2. Accessed June 23, 2021.

First, I reread a seminal essay by Pamela Miller Ness, "The Poet's Toolbox: Prosody in Haiku," first published in *Modern Haiku* 37.2. Ness explains how sound often enhances a haiku's meaning and impacts its emotional resonance: "When used with precision and subtlety, the elements of prosody such as meter, rhyme, alliteration, assonance, onomatopoeia, enjambment, and repetition can add to the musical enjoyment of the haiku while simultaneously extending the meaning and expanding the emotional resonance."[2]

Second, I reread Peggy Willis Lyles' influential book of haiku, *To Hear the Rain*. Lyles was a *maestra* at euphony. As Alan Burns writes in his introductory notes on Lyles in his anthology *Where the River Goes:* "Few haiku poets have attended so skillfully to sound as Lyles did in her finely crafted poetry."[3] As Lyles herself writes in the preface of *To Hear the Rain*: "Sound enhances meaning. Every nuance contributes to the total effect."[4] Here is one of Lyles' monoku that exhibits her mastery of euphonic techniques.

> the turning tide at standstill sandhill cranes[5]

I'm first drawn to the repetition and alliteration of the *t*- and *s*- sounds in this haiku. In addition, pronouncing

2. Ness, Pamela Miller. "The Poet's Toolbox: Prosody in Haiku." *Modern Haiku* 37.2.
3. Burns, Alan, ed. *Where the River Goes: The Nature Tradition in English-Language Haiku*. United Kingdom: Snapshot Press, 2013, 164.
4. Lyles, Peggy. *To Hear the Rain*. Decatur, IL: Brooks Books, 2002, 10.
5. Betty Drevniok Haiku Award 2008.

the near rhymes of "standstill" and then "sandhill," with the cut in between, makes me pause, perhaps like the moment just before a wave crawls back down the beach. Two more from Lyles:[6]

sun shower
the river otter
somersaults

cedar shavings
the carpenter's magnet
snaps up tacks

In the first haiku, we notice an alliteration of *s*- sounds on the first and third lines. We also hear *r*-controlled syllables ending three of the words, one in each line. In addition, all of the *s*'s and *r*'s in the poem mimic an otter undulating across the river. In the second haiku, the soft *c*- and *sh*- sounds on the first line help make that line sound soft and curly. Then the closed one-syllable words containing assonance in the last line make that line sound hard and sharp, thereby producing an effective contrast.

If we agree that these three poems "sound great," that then leads us to our first question: How do we define euphony? The definition of euphony that I prefer, believe it or not, is from *Google Dictionary*: "the quality of being pleasing to the ear, especially through a harmonious combination of words; the tendency to make phonetic change for ease of pronunciation."[7] I like this definition because of its second part, because it implies an active effort by the poet to create sound

6. Lyles, Peggy. *To Hear the Rain.*

7. *Google Dictionary*, accessed June 24, 2021.

harmony. It suggests we can, and perhaps should, create euphony in a deliberate and mindful way.

What, then, does euphony in haiku sound like? You know those moments when you read a haiku and immediately feel that it "sounds right" but can't quite put your finger on why, until you study it a bit? I think we sometimes respond positively to a haiku on an unconscious level when its word sounds are eliciting euphony. The poem sounds good in a musical way and hence feels unified. As Ness stated in her essay, euphony helps create music, extend the meaning, and expand the emotional resonance. It also helps to unify the poem.

Poetic euphony can be created in a variety of ways. Poets have traditionally written euphony into their poems by using phonemic poetic devices like rhyme, alliteration, consonance, assonance, and onomatopoeia. They also play with meter, rhythm, enjambment, repetition, and other techniques. For the purposes of this essay, I am going to focus on the phonemic devices, the ones that utilize individual sounds that make up words, and not with meter and rhythm. These sounds are referred to as phonemes, the smallest units of speech that distinguish one word from another. There are forty-four of them in the English language. The phonemes are produced by consonant sounds, vowel sounds, and combinations of consonants and vowels.

Let's take a closer look at how we can use some traditional phonemic poetic devices successfully.

Historically, haikuists have eschewed rhyme, alliteration, consonance, assonance, and onomatopoeia for some very good reasons. Using them overtly can feel heavy-handed, too clever, too contrived, too cute, or too poetic — they can distract from the haiku moment or from the poem itself. But if we use them carefully and deftly, we can create some mighty fine music. As Bashō wrote about the process of thinking about euphony during revision, ". . . a thousand times on your lips."[8]

Lee Gurga, in *Haiku: A Poet's Guide*, writes: ". . . the judicious use of aural devices in haiku can help focus the reader/listener's attention on the important aspects of the verse. Overdoing, of course, can spoil a haiku. The brief, fragile haiku is easily overwhelmed by use of powerful sounds and sound associations. The approach of the haiku poet to this problem, as to everything, requires lightness and balance."[9] If we act with lightness and balance, as Gurga suggests, these poetic devices can work successfully. As Ness asserts: "I suggest that we should actively utilize all of the musical devices available in our poet's toolboxes, though perhaps with a lighter touch given the brevity and fragility of haiku."[10]

---

8. Blyth, R.H. *Haiku Volume 1: Eastern Culture*. Japan: Hokuseido, 1949, 369.
9. Gurga, Lee. *Haiku: A Poet's Guide*. Lincoln, IL: Modern Haiku Press, 2003, 63.
10. Ness, Pamela Miller. "The Poet's Toolbox: Prosody in Haiku."

First let's consider rhyme. Many of the early translations of Japanese haiku into English rhymed. In part, that is because many Japanese words rhyme. Jane Reichhold, in *Writing and Enjoying Haiku*, states: ". . . in Japanese, due to the constructive use of vowels in the language, one has a one-in-six chance that any two lines will rhyme. Thus, the Japanese haiku often have not only a line-end rhyme but often one or more internal rhymes. The writers used this ability to strengthen their poems."[11] In English, because it is rarer to rhyme in everyday language, rhymes stick out when used in haiku, especially end rhymes. Reichhold claims that end rhymes close the haiku down, and most haiku want to leave on an open note.[12] But rhyming can work, especially internal and near rhymes, if they are done subtly. As Jim Kacian explains in his article, "The Use of Language in Haiku," "Internal and off-rhyme is a bit easier to accommodate [as opposed to end rhyme], it being less powerful and final, and a good rule of thumb is to allow rhyme or off-rhyme to stand in a poem if it comes to the poem unbidden, and does not overpower the other elements in the poem."[13] Let's look at rhyming that is successful at not overpowering the haiku. We'll examine haiku with end rhyme, internal rhyme, and near rhyme.

---

11. Reichhold, Jane. *Writing and Enjoying Haiku: A Hands-on Guide*. New York: Kodansha International, 2002, 45.
12. *Ibid*., 46
13. Kacian, Jim. "The Use of Language in Haiku." From www.poetrysociety.org.nz/affiliates/haiku-nz/haiku-poems-articles/archived-articles/the-use-of-language-in-haiku/. Accessed June 21, 2021.

End rhymes are true rhymes at the ends of lines. As noted, end rhyme is usually too heavy-handed for haiku. But there are times when it might reinforce the content. With a light touch, it can work. Sometimes end rhyme can work if one word in the pair ends with an *-s* and the other doesn't. This can occur with nouns or verbs.

> summer night
> we turn out all the lights
> to hear the rain
>
> Peggy Willis Lyles[14]

In this haiku, night and lights are near rhymes. Making one of those end words plural tweaks the poem a bit so that the end rhyme doesn't sound sing-songy. Also, the end rhymes in the first two lines tie them together so that the third line stands out. End rhyme can also be used if the lines in which they occur have different meters, as in the following poem:

> spring rain
> the measured step
> of a sandhill crane
>
> paul m.[15]

This poem is not heavy-handed, even though it contains true rhymes on lines one and three, in part because the words before the rhyming words

14. Lyles, Peggy. *To Hear the Rain.*

15. m., paul. *Witness Tree.* Edited by John Barlow. United Kingdom: Snapshot Press, 2020.

are accented differently. In line one, "spring rain" is equally accented. In line three, the word "sandhill" is a trochee, one accented syllable followed by an unaccented syllable. These different accents help to soften the rhymes.

Internal rhymes occur when there are two words that rhyme within a line, or within a haiku. According to Ness, an internal rhyme can help to unify ideas within a poem. Here's an effective example.

> morning stillness
> what's left of the mist
> shines in the pines
>
> Ben Gaa[16]

The internal rhyme in the last line helps make it resonate (and continue to shine). Internal rhymes also work well if one of the words is singular and one is plural, or one word is a verb ending with an *-s*.

> lifting fog
> every leaf tip drips
> sunlight
>
> Barbara Snow[17]

In this poem, the words "tip" and "drips" replicate the sound of the fog dripping. We can also use internal rhyme successfully on different lines, and in different positions in those lines.

16. *Wales Haiku Journal*, Winter 2021.
17. *Acorn* 45.

through the chains
of a child's swing
spring starts

Judson Evans[18]

The rhyme of "swing" at the end of line two and "spring" at the start of line three recreates the swinging action that is described in the poem. Sometimes a word can rhyme with part of another word to create euphony and unity.

sunlight
fills the millstone's furrows
a pine warbler's trill

paul m.[19]

In this poem, "fills" and "trill" rhyme with the "mill" in "millstone." In addition, the three rhymes mimic the repeated parts of a warbler's song. Note that this poem successfully combines several of the rhyming techniques we've discussed: using internal rhymes with and without an *-s*, using rhymes on different lines, and using rhymes as parts of longer words. Near rhyme occurs when words in a poem almost rhyme. This technique is also referred to as off, slant, imperfect, or approximate rhyme. As noted above, it is less intrusive and can be very effective. Ness asserts that you can create a sense of unity and closure in a poem without

18. *Frogpond* 25.2.
19. m., paul. *Witness Tree.*

the heaviness and possible sing-song quality of pure end rhyme.[20]

alone, not alone —
a loon
in still water

Ben Moeller-Gaa[21]

The repeated word "alone" in this haiku is very close to the words "a loon." The three words create an echo effect like the sound of the loon's call, adding to the emotional resonance of the poem.

winter forest
the mist
from a whisper

Connie Donleycott[22]

The words "winter" and "whisper" are near rhymes. The word "mist" is pretty close too. They all help to create unity.

flowering laurel
the hedge trimmer lowering
the sky

Michelle Schaefer[23]

The words "flowering," "lowering," and "laurel" all

20. Ness, Pamela Miller. "The Poet's Toolbox: Prosody in Haiku."

21. Moeller-Gaa, Ben. *Wishbones*. Meredith, NH: Folded Word, 2018.

22. *The Heron's Nest* 5: February 2003.

23. *Presence* 68.

sound fairly close. They bind the poem together.

Alliteration is repetition at close intervals of initial consonant sounds. Kenneth Yasuda, in his book *The Japanese Haiku*, writes: "alliteration speaks gently where rhyme commands."[24] But I would add that alliteration should also be used sparingly. David Grayson, in an essay called "Word Choice in English-Language Haiku: The Uses of Roots,"[25] writes that Anglo-Saxon words lend themselves to alliteration. In Laurence Perrine and Thomas R. Arp's book *Sound and Sense: An Introduction to Poetry*, they claim: "In addition to onomatopoetic words there is another group of words, sometimes called phonetic intensives, whose sound, by a process as yet obscure, to some degree connects to their meaning."[26]

It's intriguing to think that the sounds of the words have meaning, and not just the whole words. These intrinsic relationships of these phonemes work at the gut level. For example, initial *st-* sounds suggest strength, as in "sturdy," "steel," and, of course, "strong." Initial *sl-* sounds infer things that are "smoothly wet" as in "slippery," "slick," and "slobber." Here are examples that include these two phonetic intensives:

---

24. Yasuda, Kenneth. *The Japanese Haiku*. Rutland, VT: Charles E. Tuttle Company, 1957, 98.
25. *Frogpond* 36:1, 73.
26. Perrine, Laurence and Thomas R. Arp, *Sound and Sense: An Introduction to Poetry*. Fort Worth, TX: Harcourt Brace, 1992, 198.

the same granite
in a stile's step …
village graveyard
paul m.[27]

daylight moon
the slicked-down reeds
of a muskrat slide
Cherrie Hunter Day[28]

Alliteration is commonly used to mimic real sounds. Here's an example.

first frost
the echo of the caw
of the crow
Mark Hollingsworth[29]

Here the repeated hard *c*- sounds mimic the call of the crow. And the word "crow" is a close echo of the sound of a caw. Alliteration can also emphasize quantity, since repeated instances of a particular sound allude to a greater number of a particular item in the poem, as in the number of leaves in a pile.

light
on the pile
last autumn leaf
Jeannie Martin[30]

This poem is a pile of *l* sounds. Are you ready to dive in? Alliteration can work seamlessly if there are other words in between the words with alliterative sounds.

---

27. m., paul. *Witness Tree.*
28. *The Heron's Nest* 16:4.
29. *Frogpond* 32:3.
30. *Acorn* 43.

a change in their voices ...
children finding
a fledgling

John Stevenson[31]

The *ch-* sounds on lines one and two and the *f-* sounds on lines two and three connect to create unity. The alliteration is not in back-to-back words—there are words in between that prevent it from sounding like a tongue twister.

Kenneth Yasuda, in *The Japanese Haiku*, talks about what he calls "oblique alliteration," which is the "repetition of the same initial consonant sound followed by a different consonant sound."[32] This can be created by using words that start with different consonant blends, like *sm-*, *sw-*, *st-*, *sp-*, etc. He claims that you can use oblique alliteration to produce "similarity" instead of "exactness."

sleet storm
the bare tree branches glisten
with grackles

Brenda J. Gannam[33]

In this poem, we find the *sl-* and *st-* in line one, and the *gl-* and *gr-* in lines two and three, examples of oblique alliteration that help to unify the poem. Yasuda also

31. *The Heron's Nest* 4:11.
32. Yasuda, Kenneth. *The Japanese Haiku.*
33. *The Heron's Nest* 10:1.

discusses what he calls "crossed alliteration."[34] This is a more complex version of alliteration. This happens when sets of alliteration alternate, as in a chain.

a beer can
for comparison
bear paw print

Carolyn Hall[35]

In Hall's haiku, "beer" and "bear" alternate with "can" and "comparison."

billowing clouds
a spittle bug claims
the daisy stem

Julie Warther[36]

In this poem, there seem to be three links in the chain. "Billowing" and "bug," "clouds" and "claims," and "spittle" and "stem" all take turns alternating.

Consonance is similar to alliteration, but the repetition of consonant sounds is found in the medial or end positions of words. Gurga asserts that consonance is, "less dominating than alliteration."[37] It's certainly more subtle.

---

34. Yasuda, Kenneth. *The Japanese Haiku*, 103-104.
35. Hall, Carolyn. *Cricket Dusk*. Winchester, VA: Red Moon Press, 2020.
36. *Presence* 58.
37. Gurga, Lee. *Haiku: A Poet's Guide*, 65.

still wet
the gravestones sparkle
grackles

Chuck Brickley[38]

This example includes medial consonance: the *k* sounds in the middle of "sparkle" and "grackle."

last light
black ducks forage
for acorns

Kristen Lindquist[39]

Lindquist's poem includes end consonance: the *-ck* at the end of "black" and "ducks." According to Perrine and Arp, these phonetic intensives suggest quick movement.[40]

new moon
the night watchman
goes unseen

Scott Mason[41]

Here, the repeated ending *-n* sounds give it extra emotional resonance and remind me of the repeated rounds of a night watchman. This consonance adds to the meaning of the poem.

---

38. *Frogpond* 44:1.
39. *Seabeck Getaway 2020 Anthology*, forthcoming.
40. Perrine, Laurence and Thomas R. Arp, *Sound and Sense: An Introduction to Poetry*, 199.
41. Mason, Scott. *The Wonder Code*. Chappaqua, NY: Girasole Press, 2017.

dusk
to darkness
meadow to wood

John Stevenson[42]

The consonance in this haiku is intriguing and deftly performed. The *d-* sound starts as initial alliteration, then transforms into medial and terminal consonance. This creates an effect not unlike the transition from day into night.

Assonance, the repetition at close intervals of vowel sounds, is what Ness calls "vowel rhyme."[43] Gurga writes that assonance is "usually the least obtrusive of the aural devices."[44] He further states that it can reinforce a theme without drawing attention to itself.[45] I think assonance is perhaps the most effective unifier of the more traditional euphonic devices.

morning crescent
rising from the glen
the scent of wild fennel

Chuck Brickley[46]

Here we hear the short *e* sounds in four different words, "crescent," "glen," "scent," and "fennel." The repeated sounds help to conjure up wafts of fennel scent.

42. *Upstate Dim Sum* 2019/I.
43. Ness, Pamela Miller. "The Poet's Toolbox: Prosody in Haiku."
44. Gurga, Lee. *Haiku: A Poet's Guide*, 65.
45. *Ibid.*
46. *Frogpond* 44:2.

spring equinox
the cyclist's thighs
scissoring sunlight

Mary Stevens[47]

In this poem, we hear the alternating short and long *i* sounds, like the cyclist's thighs pedaling up and down.

Onomatopoeia is a word that, through its sound as well as its sense, represents what it defines.[48] William Higginson, in *The Haiku Handbook*, claims that "onomatopoeia dramatically unifies a poem."[49] Many names of instruments and birds are onomatopoeic, and they are welcome in haiku.

taut tent
the tympani
of rain

Jim Kacian[50]

Here the name of a musical instrument is onomatopoeic. Kacian also throws in a few more *t*- sounds to emphasize the beat of the tympani.

---

47. *Kingfisher* 1.
48. Oliver, Mary. *A Poetry Handbook*. New York: Harcourt, Brace & Co., 1994, 32.
49 Higginson, William. *The Haiku Handbook*. New York: Kodansha International, 1985, 126.
50. Welch, Michael Dylan and Crystal Simone Smith, Editors. *Sitting in the Sun*. Sammamish, WA: Press Here, 2019.

a peewee keeps calling
the deep roots
of weeds

Allan Burns[51]

The peewee bird is named for its call, hence it acts as onomatopoeia. Burns helps to repeat the peewee's call by using the assonance of the long e sounds in "keeps," "deep," and "weeds."

We have seen that traditional poetic sound devices can be used quite successfully in haiku. In my study of haiku that exhibit euphony, I've noticed some other less traditional, but very effective, sound devices. Lyles, in the preface to *To Hear the Rain*, writes that one characteristic of all poetry is ". . . careful diction with close attention to the denotations, connotations, and associative possibilities of words."[52] I've found eight other euphonic poetic devices that utilize euphonic denotations, connotations, and associations. I call them Intra-Line Unity, Euphonic Contrast, Completing the Circle, Mash-Up, Moonlighting, Shadow Words, Nesting Dolls, and Anagrams. Let's examine how each of them work.

Sometimes each line of a haiku uses a distinctive sound device, thereby creating its own euphonic thread or intra-line unity.

---

51. Burns, Allan. *Distant Virga*. Winchester, VA: Red Moon Press, 2011.
52. Lyles, Peggy. *To Hear the Rain*.

patio tai chi
a hummingbird's quick sip
at the coral bells

Julie Warther[53]

In line one, we hear the t sounds and the long e sounds. In line two, we hear two closed syllable words with short i sounds at the very end. In line three, we hear the consonance of "coral" and "bells." Each line has its own unifying characteristic that helps to create total poem unity as well.

Sometimes two of the lines in a haiku share a common euphonic thread, while a third line does not, and this can create an effective juxtaposition of sound and mood. Such intra-line unity can be used to create euphonic contrast in a haiku. For example, the last line can sound different than the first two, as in this haiku:

death notice
daylilies divided
for another garden

Michele Root-Bernstein[54]

The first two lines of this haiku are full of *d-* sounds. At present, the garden in the poem is the one with daylilies (symbolized by *d-* sounds). The third line does not contain any initial *d-* sounds, because the prospective garden has yet to receive the transplanted day lilies. The repeated *d-* sounds help to intensify the

53. *Hedgerow* 119.

54. Haiku Poets of Northern California Haiku Contest 2012.

sadness in the poem. Sometimes, the line that stands on its own is the first one:

honeysuckle
we open jelly jars
for fireflies

Peggy Willis Lyles[55]

The first line in this haiku is the only one without alliteration. Then we get to the *j*- alliteration in line two and the *f*- alliteration in line three. So the first line is the one that stands out.

Euphony can also be used to "complete the circle" in a haiku. Sometimes, a haiku feels unified because, in fact, it has been deliberately unified by the use of near rhymes in the first and last words of the poem. The circle of the haiku moment gets cinched, and this can be very emotionally satisfying.

last year's hostas
our losses
turn to lace

Peter Newton[56]

The near rhymes of "last" and "lace" allude to the cycles of growth during the year. This haiku also includes the near rhymes of "hostas" and "losses," to add to the poem's resonance.

---

55. Lyles, Peggy Willis. *To Hear the Rain.*

56. Mason, Scott, Editor. *Gratitude in the Time of COVID-19.* Chappaqua, NY: Girasole Press, 2020.

lilac petals
the wind turns
italic

Chad Lee Robinson[57]

In this poem, "lilac" and "italic" are near rhymes. One could also picture the wind scattering the letters in the word "lilac" to form the word "italic."

A couple of years ago, I started to notice a euphonic process that I was engaging in during my writing, first unconsciously, then more deliberately. I create one part of a haiku, usually the phrase, and then let its sounds, in an almost instinctual way, lead me to associative sounds for the fragment. To do this, I repeat the phrase in my head or out loud, listening to its sounds, shuffling those sounds around, and seeing what tumbles out. The process feels a bit like I am creating a mash-up song, hence I call the poetic device "Mash-Up." Here's a haiku that emerged out of this process.

waxing moon
fiddler crabs mob
the mud flats

Brad Bennett[58]

I wrote this while visiting Cape Cod. I was looking for the perfect verb to describe the movement of the crabs and I was considering "crawl" and a few other words. I kept reading the words in the poem over to myself.

57. *Acorn* 34.
58. *Mariposa* 41.

Somehow, the *-b* sound in "crab" and the *m-* sound in "mud" made me think of the word "mob." I thought it fit well euphonically and added to the unity of the poem.

We all know that a word in a haiku can do more than one job. Perhaps helping to depict the haiku moment is a word's day job. The same word, though, can moonlight — it can pick up another job. It can also add euphony and/or emotional resonance to the poem. Often there is one important word in a haiku that is doing the most moonlighting. Here are two examples of this phenomenon.

a jay stuffs more seeds
into its esophagus
last days of summer

Brad Bennett[59]

In my first draft, I used the word "crop," which I thought was the accurate word to describe the storage space in a bird's throat. But I didn't like the sound of it. So, I did some research online and found out that it's not actually a crop that the jay is using as a storage container, it's actually using a part of its esophagus. The word "esophagus" was the accurate word, and it also gave me two more *s* sounds and another *f* sound to create more poem unity. I also imagined that the extra *s*'s were being stored in the word "esophagus." So, the word performed several jobs in my haiku.

59. Unpublished.

street bazaar
the wind lifts a tune
from a terracotta pot

Alan S. Bridges[60]

I don't know the history of how Bridges constructed this poem. But he could have used many different descriptors for the pot. The word "terracotta" sounds like a tune the wind might make blowing into or over a pot, so the word served several purposes in the poem: descriptive, semantic, and euphonic.

When we read a haiku, we make connections to memories, emotions, and prior knowledge. We may also make connections to other words that are not even present in the haiku. I've noticed that occasionally a word or a pair of words in a haiku makes me think of another word not in the haiku. The first word and its context can lead me to another word that might sound similar, but is not there. I think this can happen consciously or unconsciously. I call these words "shadow words."[61] Here are a few examples.

soft serve at the wharf
a sloop coming in
on evening wind

Hannah Mahoney[62]

---

60. Kaji Aso Haiku Contest 2020.

61 Mary Stevens and I first noticed this phenomenon while workshopping together. The term "shadow word" was coined by Kristen Lindquist during a subsequent conversation.

62. *Acorn* 45.

In this poem, the word “sloop” and the fact that we’re being treated to ice cream, led me to think of the word “scoop.” When I took a closer look, I saw the sound and context connection.

April drizzle . . .
the long wait
for fried clams

Jim Laurila[63]

In this poem, the word “drizzle,” and the implied sound of clams frying in oil, reminded me of the word “sizzle.” Mahoney and Laurila did not deliberately include these words in these contexts in order to trigger the other words that came to my mind, but it happened nonetheless, and I would argue that it adds semantic meaning to these haiku. Sometimes, I deliberately create a situation where another word might emerge in a reader’s mind. Here’s an example:

creek trickle
a chickadee lands
on my hand

Brad Bennett[64]

I used the word “trickle” in hopes that the word “tickle” might fly into a reader’s mind. Perhaps like the chickadee’s feet tickling my palm.

---

63. Unpublished.
64. *New England Letters* 107.

The sounds of word parts can interact in interesting ways. For instance, you can use one word by itself and also as a syllable or part of another longer word. This repetition can create an effect like "nesting dolls" that helps to produce more euphony, unity, and resonance.

> snow wind
> wringing the tea bag
> until it tears
>
> Robert Gilliland[65]

In this poem, "tea" is nested in "tear." The alliteration in the words "tea" and "tear" is also very effective, especially since the second word is altered by just one letter, perhaps like a tea bag being torn open.

> a cold cup
> from a cold cupboard
> morning sun
>
> Peggy Willis Lyles[66]

This haiku does something intriguing. The word "cup" is repeated, but the *p*- sound is lost in the word cupboard. This one feels like the cups are nesting, one inside the other.

In some haiku, the letters and sounds in a word or phrase from one line can be used to create a related word with similar sounds in another line. The letters and sounds get rearranged in a way that reminds me of anagrams.

---

65. *Frogpond* 26:2.
66. *Acorn* 20.

summer dusk
a duck's wake
turns back the waves

Madelaine Caritas Longman[67]

If you take four of the letters in "duck's" and scramble them, you can form the word "dusk." So, the second line gives us a new way to create the "dusk" that was introduced in the first line.

sunlit silt the marsh rabbit's eyes

Kristen Lindquist[68]

If you rearrange some of the letters in "sunlit," you get "silt." That word pair is also an example of near rhyme.

As we've seen, there are many intriguing and intricate ways that phonemes can be played to great effect in our haiku. As long as they are used carefully, deftly, and creatively, they can produce euphony that is not too sing-songy, too heavy-handed, or too forced. The resulting music can sound quite pleasing and create resonance and unity. As Pamela Miller Ness reminds us, ". . . we need to write with our ears as well as our eyes and minds."[69]

first awake a lake of mist

John Stevenson[70]

---

67. *Modern Haiku* 51.3.
68. *Wales Haiku Journal*, Autumn 2021.
69. Ness, Pamela Miller. "The Poet's Toolbox: Prosody in Haiku."
70. *Upstate Dim Sum* 2019/I.

Acknowledgements

The author would like to thank Hannah Mahoney for suggesting the word "euphony" to describe what the devices examined in this essay produce in haiku. Many thanks also go to those who invited him to give Zoom presentations of earlier versions of this essay: Haiku Waukesha, Ohai-o Haiku Study Group, Seabeck Haiku Getaway 2020, Evergreen Haiku Study Group, Poetry Pea, and Haiku Poets of Northern California. Finally, the author is grateful to Chuck Brickley, Alan Bridges, Gary Hotham, Kristen Lindquist, Hannah Mahoney, Scott Mason, Mary Stevens, and Michael Dylan Welch, for their assistance with understanding the concepts elucidated in this essay.

David Burleigh ✧ Ireland/Japan

Haiku: Who's Counting?

When the environmental activist Greta Thunberg sailed into New York Harbor, her boat was met by a flotilla of other vessels, seventeen in all, each representing by its numbered sail one of the demands to be made at a conference on climate change. When I receive a gift of *sembei*, large crunchy rice crackers, from Sōka, the first place that Bashō stopped after leaving Edo on his journey to the North, there are seventeen inside the box, of different sizes, and I wonder if the number has any meaning. In Art Spiegelman's graphic novel *Maus*, just when his father has entered a concentration camp and is losing hope, a priest looks at the tattoo on his arm, and says: "Your number starts with 17. In Hebrew that's *k'minyan tov*. Seventeen is a very good omen."[1] Fortune shows that the bearer will survive, and overcome adversity, as of course he does, or we wouldn't have the story. Is there, then, some magic in the number?

Haiku poets in Japan often invoke the number seventeen, of course, that being the one that indicates the form of haiku, and it doesn't really matter whether

1. Spiegelman, Art. *Maus: A Survivor's Tale II—And Here My Troubles Began*. New York: Pantheon Books, 1991, p. 28.

you call the counted parts syllables, *onji*, or morae, the sum total is the same. It is a prime number, more rhythmical in English than any of those adjacent to it, which may be why Billy Collins chose it for the title of his small book from Modern Haiku Press, *She Was Just Seventeen* (2006): 'eleven' clearly wouldn't be the same. Numerology, at least of the Biblical kind, is not invoked in the book's beautiful design, though the cover does carry the Chinese hexagram for that number, playfully suggesting divination, and it appears again by the epigraph inside, in all its suggestive mystery. More mundanely, I noticed that some paired short verses by a literary scholar, printed in the *London Review of Books* a couple of years ago, were all in the pattern of 5-7-5 syllables, though without any other appreciable poetic quality. What this might mean, or what it might say about the reception of haiku as an English poetic form, is the subject I would like to consider.

Most dictionaries and reference books mention seventeen syllables, in a pattern of 5-7-5, as well as saying something about nature, in defining 'haiku' as an English word. In Japanese there are two words, pronounced identically: 俳句, meaning 'haiku' composed in Japanese, and ハイク, meaning 'haiku' in other languages or scripts, a clear visual distinction that can be useful in book or essay titles, to show the transition from one to the other, for example, or discuss the global spread of the poetic form. In English, and especially in the popular imagination, the numbers are what define the form. A new volume of translations of Bashō, put out by the Buddhist Society in London, has "5-7-5" on its cover,[2] while another volume due to come out in America next year will, I'm told, render the whole of the poet's work in English syllabic form. For haiku aficionados who compose originally in English, this is now often not the case. Indeed I was once told myself that composing syllabically is 'wrong.'

I do not think that, in poetry, there is a 'right' or 'wrong' way, only that some things seem to work, and others not to, for reasons that are complex and mysterious. The best that can be said of a poem is that it 'works,' something we can often recognize without knowing exactly why or how it happens. It is not a prescriptive matter of following the rules, which are often broken. The default pattern in English prosody is the iambic pentameter, perhaps, but a wholly regular beat soon becomes tedious and ineffective. Breaking the rhythm creates interest or freshness, and so it is sometimes too with the 5-7-5 rhythm in Japanese. Yet the idea — which I have heard quite categorically stated — that English is 'metrical' and Japanese is 'syllabic,' is much too simple. Thom Gunn's masterly short poem, "Considering the Snail," composed in heptasyllabic (7-syllable) lines, is plainly both. Even free verse carries the ghost of the formal pattern that it departed from, because poetry must have some kind of rhythm. The verses of the free-

2. White, John, & Kemmyo Taira Sato. *5-7-5 The Haiku of Bashō.* London: The Buddhist Society Trust, 2019. A volume of Issa has appeared, in the same format. I wonder what they will do if they go on to Santōka?

form haiku poet Santōka are likewise ghosted by the Japanese tradition out of which they came.

All of the poets who won the Nobel Prize for Literature and dabbled in haiku (Seferis, Paz, Heaney, Tränstromer) used the regular form. Another laureate, Dag Hammarskjöld, who was posthumously awarded the Peace Prize, did so too, although W.H. Auden reprised the strict 5-7-5 of the Swedish originals into a more flexible total of seventeen in his English versions. Apart from Paz, all of these poets are European, and I have often noted how the form persists in poetry journals and collections in Britain and Ireland. Frank Ormsby (b. 1947), who lives in Belfast and is currently Ireland Professor of Poetry, has included sequences of such verses, under the title "Small World," in his last four collections. And in an anthology of living poets facing off with dead ones (in which Billy Collins addresses W.H. Auden), the British poet Imtiaz Dharker (b. 1954) takes on Rumi, in a loosely composed poem entitled "Myth," that resolves on the second page into a sequence of syllabic verses: "The mist of my breath / slides off the angled mirror / to reveal your face."[3] In the same poet's collection, *Luck is the Hook* (2018), there are several three-line verses, all with titles, and some precisely in the syllabic form.

There is notable tendency, it seems to me, among the poets who use the syllabic pattern, to create a verse

3. Duffy, Carol Ann, ed. *Answering Back: Living Poets Reply to Poems from the Past*. London: Picador, 2007, pp. 54-55. After three more, the last one ends: "My heart grows immense."

that is something of a puzzle, but that also arguably has the playful quality of *haikai*, out of which the haiku originally came. Here is another by Imtiaz Dharker:

> Light falls from the sky
> like a fresh sheet on a bed
> you will not sleep in.
>
> ("Made, Unmade")[4]

In a similar but slightly more macabre vein, the late Matthew Sweeney, an Irish poet, has a few such verses in his collection *A Smell of Fish* (2000), for example:

> I catch jellyfish
> and leave them on the tarmac
> to swim in the rain.
>
> ("Hobby")[5]

This exercise extended to the novel Sweeney composed with his fellow English poet, John Hartley Williams.

The novel, called *Death Comes for the Poets* (2012), is a murder mystery and sends up the poetry scene in Britain, a world of readings and small journals, of editing and workshops and hard-won meager sales. Both of the authors were working poets, and knew all this intimately. The plot is built around a series of murders, and there are jokes about poetic practice, including haiku. At the end of the book there is a rather brilliant brief anthology of the poets' work,

4. Dharker, Imtiaz. *Luck is the Hook*. UK: Bloodaxe Books, 2018, p. 35.
5. Sweeney, Matthew. *A Smell of Fish*. London: Jonathan Cape, 2000, p. 36.

with individual faux creations for all of the characters. Their names are arranged alphabetically, from Anita Bellows, through Fergus Diver, Damian Krapp, and Melinda Speling, to the seventeenth and final poet, Manfred Von Zitzewitz, who writes only haiku, and so the book closes with this verse:

> The white stallion
> galloped along the runway
> to meet the airplane
>
> ("Glad")[6]

It is not of course what we usually expect of 'haiku,' but withal it is a poem, and subsequently appeared in one of Matthew Sweeney's own collections. It is all quite entertaining, but what are we to make of it?

Although the same two poets jointly authored a practical guide, *Teach Yourself Writing Poetry* (2003), for a popular series, and this too has many improvised examples, haiku is never mentioned in that volume. It does, however, take a central role in another novel, a bestseller by the distinguished British novelist Ian McEwan, *Machines Like Me* (2019). This futurist tale, actually set in the 1970s, features a robot called Adam, which is bought by the protagonist and then falls in love with his human girlfriend. Alan Turing is still alive, and appears later in the story to deliver sage remarks:

6. Sweeney, Matthew & John Hartley Williams. *Death Comes For the Poets*. London: Muswell Press, 2012, p. 313. The book is dedicated to the mythical Australian poet Ern Malley, the subject of a famous literary hoax.

> "The other day, Thomas reminded me of the famous Latin tag from Virgil's *Aeneid. Sunt lacrimae rerum* — there are tears in the nature of things. None of us knows how to encode that perception."[7]

The debate here is about whether the most delicate human feelings and perceptions (*mono no aware*) can be electronically reproduced, and the answer so far is that AI is not quite equal to the task. Nevertheless, Adam continues to work on his "haikus," and the few examples included, all of them syllabic, do not undermine this argument.[8] But for haiku aficionados the focus lies elsewhere.

The development from syllabic patterns, to freer and usually shorter forms of composition, is easy enough to see in representative anthologies, like those edited by Cor van den Heuvel, or *Haiku in English: The First Hundred Years*,[9] to which I shall return. Even so, I notice that a new book on James W. Hackett, a devotee of the regular syllabic pattern, by Paul Russell Miller,[10] has seventeen chapters, which can hardly be accidental. Be that as it may, I would like at this point to go further back, to a small but ambitiously pioneering anthology edited by George Swede and

7. McEwan, Ian. *Machines Like Me*. London: Vintage, 2020, p. 180.

8. It is notable that in Kazuo Ishiguro's new novel, *Klara and the Sun* (2021), which is also about a robot companion, haiku is never mentioned.

9. Kacian, Jim, Philip Rowland & Allan Burns, eds. *Haiku in English: The First Hundred Years*. New York: W.W. Norton, 2013.

10. Miller, Paul Russell. *The Wild Beyond Echoing: James Hackett's Haiku Way*. Painswick, UK: Grandad Publishing, 2021.

Randy Brooks, called *Global Haiku: Twenty-five Poets World-wide* (2000),[11] that came out from a small press in Canada. The focus was narrow, and it was carelessly proofed, but its title announced a larger movement or awareness of haiku as the century was about to turn. Whether the chosen poets remain significant is not the point, but rather that the focus had grown. Furthermore, the generous Foreword to the book by the late Makoto Ueda gestured toward some greater potential recognition, in comparing the haiku to the sonnet. I was rather startled by this.

This is not to suggest that Professor Ueda's remarks were uninformed or ill considered in any way, but only that the sonnet has a long history and a well-established position as a poetic form, with many illustrious practitioners, in comparison to which the haiku can still appear novel, and quite slight. The process of adaptation is a slow one, as Ueda says, and it took a century or more for the sonnet to find its place. The new shape that emerged in English had at first either longer or shorter lines than the Italian original, and often simpler rhymes. The 'English' or Shakespearean sonnet turned into three quatrains and a couplet, instead of an octave and a sestet, but still added up to fourteen lines. Since then the form has been played with in all kinds of ways, though the basic idea has remained the same. An anthology that I have to hand, *The Art of the Sonnet* by Stephen Burt and

---

11. Swede, George & Randy Brooks, eds. *Global Haiku: Twenty-five Poets World-wide*. Ontario: Mosaic Press, 2000.

David Mikics (2010),[12] gives a hundred examples, from the earliest poets to the present, covering 450 years, and shows how much the form has been stretched and altered in that time, while still retaining an essential shape. Notably, three of the poets in this book also appear in *Haiku in English: The First Hundred Years*. One of them is Wallace Stevens, while the other two are Seamus Heaney and Paul Muldoon, both Irish.

While Seamus Heaney's modest offerings in the haiku form are few in number in his published collections, Paul Muldoon has been much more prolific, though both cleave to the syllabic pattern. Muldoon has played extensively with the sonnet, employing it as a stanza in some of his longer compositions, though he likes to say that it is not he who 'plays with the form,' but rather that the form 'plays' with him. The "Hopefield Haiku" in *Hay* (1998) are a dazzling technical achievement, while the *Sixty Instant Messages to Tom Moore* (2005), published by Modern Haiku Press in a beautifully designed small book, became "90 Instant Messages . . ." in the poet's next collection,[13] so that the earlier version is likely to become a collector's item. What this might show of how the haiku has turned into an essential part of mainstream poetry (and there are plenty of poets who do not write sonnets) is hard to discern. But the form pops up again briefly in Paul Muldoon's most

---

12. Burt, Stephen & David Mikics, eds. *The Art of the Sonnet*. Cambridge, Mass.: Belnap Press, 2010.
13. Muldoon, Paul. *Horse Latitudes*. London: Faber & Faber, 2006, pp. 53-75.

recent volume, *Howdie-Skelp* (2021). The single verse in question, so wittily off-hand, is called "Chipmunk."[14]

It is difficult to write like Muldoon without sounding like him, so distinctive is his style, but the casual tone belies the careful thematic pattern of each book. He has used the 5-7-5 pattern before to describe animals, which also come in elsewhere in this collection. Oddly enough, the same is repeatedly true of a sequence of 17-syllable verses by the Scottish poet Robert Crawford (b. 1959) that appeared in the *LRB* in February 2021. It is given in the list of contents as a "Poem," and consists of sixty-six numbered verses, in eighteen uneven sections, with the title "Old World," and a double-page spread.[15] It has an epigraph from Matthew Arnold that invokes the "green earth" before cultivation began to change it, suggesting a theme of environmental destruction, and a verse in the last section reprises one from the early part of Bashō's journey to the North: "'Art's origins lie / Deep in the farming songs / of seed-time.' (Bashō)."[16] The poet's name has been added to meet the syllable-count. Some of the verses, a little less than half, are in italics. All are evenly syllabic.

---

14. Muldoon, Paul. *Howdie-Skelp*. London: Faber & Faber, 2021, p. 110. There is another chipmunk in the shorter syllabic sequence, "News Headlines from the Homer Noble Farm", in Muldoon's earlier collection, *Moy Sand and Gravel*. New York: Farrar, Strauss and Giroux, 2002, p. 55.
15. Crawford, Robert. "Old World". *London Review of Books*, 4 February 2021, pp. 34-35.
16. "Old World", XVIII, 64, p. 35.

Whether Robert Crawford's long sequence constitutes a major work is hard to tell. It is freighted with a strong environmental message, some of it expressed in the same kind of humorous verses described above: "Each morning to wash, / I pack my trunk with water / Then hose myself down."[17] Along with the elephant, anteaters, bees, and bats make an appearance in this guessing game, as do giraffes and albatrosses, pandas and polar bears. It is rather didactic, though 'light' is offered as a ray of hope in various guises, including the light of the moon, so beloved of the poet Bashō, in the closing section. It is not easy to see all this going very far, but the continued use of the syllabic form needs to be acknowledged as one part of the expanding influence of haiku on English poetics. It is still around, as a lingering phantom. The last poet in *Haiku in English: The First Hundred Years*, Rebecca Lilly, though her poems there are short, quite often composes in a total of seventeen, as Auden did. The 2020 Tokyo Olympics ran officially for seventeen days, even though some events took place before it opened. And Ōtani Shōhei, the two-way baseball star of the Los Angeles Angels, who was named MVP for 2021, plays under the number 17.

---

17. "Old World", IV, 16, p. 34. As if to confirm the tendency suggested here, the same journal has just published a poem called "Pine Processionaries" by A.E. Stallings, an American poet resident in Greece, consisting of seventeen verses in the 5-7-5 syllabic form. *London Review of Books*, 27 January 2022, p. 24.

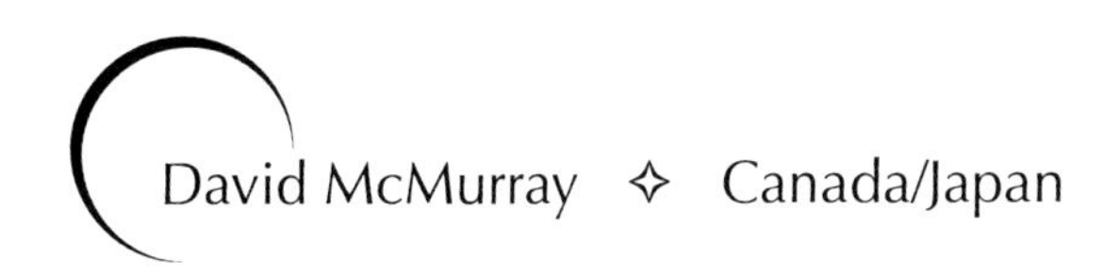

Matsuo Basho's Influence on Haiku

Haiku topics today are out of kilter from hokku penned in the past. This is what Blyth (1949) meant in warning that "there is the danger of reading into the verse meaning which the age had not attained to" (p. 337). Some parts of Japan continue to be lucky enough to have four distinct seasons, though in Akita Prefecture where Bashō once traveled, the spring and autumn seem to last shorter than before; whereas, the winter and summer are much longer and harsher. So long as there are four seasons in Japan, haikuists would likely continue to follow the season words that Basho used (Uedo, 1992). But the times and global climate conditions are changing.

A historical comparison of language change can be inferred by observing when Matsuo Bashō visited Kisakata on the west coast of the Tohoku region in 1689 (Barnhill, 2005). He viewed a shoreline as beautiful as Matsushima Bay on the Pacific side to the East and penned: *yūbare ya sakura ni suzumu nami no hana.*

Clearing at evening —
cool under the cherry trees
blossoms on the waves

The lovely Kisakata Bay, however, was completely filled in by an earthquake that hit in 1804. Over a century after Bashō's visit, Kobayashi Issa revered it in 1811 with this haiku: *kisagata o naku-nakushi keri kirigirisu.*

> Crickets cry
> as they lose it all—
> Kisakata

The landscape of Kisakata on the west coast of the Tohoku region (on the Sea of Japan) seen by Bashō and Issa can be better appreciated when contrasted with works on the east coast today. Thankfully, Matsushima Bay narrowly escaped being destroyed by a March 11, 2011, earthquake, and resulting tsunami and nuclear meltdown. It can be argued that the cause of the earthquake was geothermal, and the resulting tsunami disaster was not manmade. However, man's current pursuit of oil by fracking methods has induced earthquakes. Fracking, a drilling process that injects millions of liters of water, sand and chemicals under high pressure into a well, cracking the rock to release natural gas and oil, can cause earthquakes and tremors. Because global warming is shortening spring, haikuists may have to dare to coin new seasonal references such as fracking.

The study of language change is referred to as historical linguistics. Traditionally, scholars studied just the origins of language and the overall differences in the sounds of the language through the ages. From the early 20th century until our present time, most language changes have been syntactic, the meaning of words and sociolinguistics. The haiku example below contains these elements. Coining haiku that includes phrases such as "meltdown" are achieved by combining an understanding of traditional Japanese thinking with an accepted modern English format. For many haikuists in Tohoku such as Yutaka Kitajima, the words radiation leaks and meltdown (from nuclear meltdown) have been codified among spring season words.

Eastern wind —
radiation leaks
in silence

In addition to historical linguistics, haiku pedagogy inspired by Matsuo Bashō is applied in diverse learning environments. Basho's haiku teaching is often quoted as mindfulness training (Wawrytko, 2013). A banana tree planted beside the hut where he lived inspired his haiku name: Bashō. It was a simple tree which he apparently cherished because he wrote in his travel journal "Being completely useless as wood for building, it never feels the ax" (Wawrytko, 2013, p. 145). Matsuo Bashō (1966, 1985) also brush-stroked a flower and wrote this three-line verse verse:

There beside the road,
A hibiscus and a horse
Has chewed it all up

What is striking about his haiga, a sketch-poem, is how the painting differed from the poem. There is no horse to be seen. Instead the focus is on the hibiscus which is about to disappear. Leon Zolbrod (1982), a scholar and translator of Japanese literature and history, offered this detailed description of the painting that allows us to visualize its aesthetics:

> The overall composition has grace and simplicity with the barest minimum of color — pale rose and a dark olive that borders on gray. The calligraphic text at the top runs from the upper left toward the lower right, the reverse of the normal right to left pattern. The line of vision moves from the lower right to upper left, from where the text brings it back toward the center to an imaginary point, or boundary, between text and picture. The seal impression is placed slightly aslant, emphasizing the symmetry of asymmetry, an established aesthetic principle in East Asian painting and calligraphy. A few deft strands of grass in the lower right-hand corner introduce a contrastive element. Parallel as a common everyday image to the horse, which is mentioned in the verse but is not represented in the picture. (cited in Wawrytko, 2013, p. 237)

To motivate haiku pedagogy on the campus where I study haiku, I invited a group of Australian poets to visit the International University of Kagoshima. They had been to see the Yamadera Bashō Memorial Museum collection. It is a modestly-sized but expertly presented museum that affords an intimate glimpse of the great poet's life and writings. The aims I have for my own international haiku class are three-fold: (1) to introduce students to the fascinating paths in which haiku has spread around the world, (2) to encourage them to compose their own haiku in English at Asahi Haikuist Network and (3) enlist their support for putting haiku on the UNESCO list of intangible world heritage.

The Australian haikuists' journey took them from Tokyo to Yamagata, heading north in Basho's footsteps, never travelling far on any day. Bashō's journey, which covered a far greater distance, ended in Ogaki six months after he had set out, at which point his journal concludes. But it is worth noting that, although travelling in dangerous times, Bashō spent more than two and a half years on the road before returning to Edo (Tokyo) in 1691.

When I introduced my class of international haiku students to Beverley George (2016), the past president of the Australian Haiku Society, the students read some of her Bashō inspired poetry. This haiku by George won the Kusamakura International Haiku Competition, held in Kumamoto. It was directly inspired by Bashō.

> tsunami dreams
> grass pillows for the homeless
> on Bashō's narrow road

The invited guests from Australia shared stories with the Japanese students of how they sat at Bashō's fire, walked in summer grasses where he wrote of soldiers' dreams, and saw his cloak and pilgrim hat. They suggested it was a great privilege for all visitors—both Japanese and non-Japanese. These words penned by Basho as he set off on his journey *Oku no Hosomichi* continue to inspire journeys, especially through rural Japan:

> *"I myself have been tempted for a long time by the cloud-moving wind—filled with a strong desire to wander."* (Matsuo Bashō, 1985, p. 53).

Here is another example of a haiku that was inspired from Bashō:

> Summer moon—
> light echoes across
> the canyon

It was widely republished and appeared online at several places such as the *Akita International Haiku Network, Daily Haiku-Haiga*, and *Triveni Haikai India*. In a review of the haiku on Charlotte Digregorio's blog, Paul Beech commented; "And I hear echoes of Bashō in this haiku of David McMurray's! Brilliant. With its bold artwork and stunning verse, this haiga from David McMurray is truly compelling." Donna Bauerly said; "What a marvel of synesthesia!" Synesthesia is the experience of hearing music, but seeing shapes: The experience of one sense through another.

Other comments included Marcie Wells: "I like the mix of senses in this one — light echoes is very beautiful." "Nani Mariani commented: "I could feel the reflection of LIGHT in the canyon." Kanji Dev suggested: "The combination of imagery and sound in this haiku is quite haunting! The steep walls and the bouncing echo made the hairs on my spine stand on end. The results are amazing."

The above summer moon haiku was originally published in *A Hundred Gourds* and was inserted alongside Beverley George's (2016) article "In the footsteps of Bashō: small group travel in Japan with a focus on Japanese literature" (p. 2). Unlike Bashō, who burnt moxa on his shins to give him strength, haikuists today travel by comfortable coach. Her pilgrimage started from the site of Bashō's small hut with a banana tree beside the Sumida River, given to him by his pupils. Bashō's name was Matsuo Kinsaku. His *go* (pen-name) came from that of a plant, a type of plantain, that did not bear fruit but whose broad leaves shredded in the wind. Bashō likely drew a personal parallel with this and the single life of a wandering poet.

The Australian group comprised haiku poets and a travel writer. All were avid readers. Several were first-time visitors to Japan. By the end of their journey, every traveler had felt moved to express some impressions of their journey in haiku, and several also in haiga.

Bashō museum
watching and listening
the ripples widen

The above haiku was penned by David Terelinck, Biggera Waters, Queensland while on a visit to Japan to see the Bashō memorials.

my feet
too small to fit
Bashō's sandals

The above haiku was penned by Jo Tregellis, Cooranbong, New South Wales while on a visit to Japan to see Bashō memorials.

Travelers to Japan can learn about Japanese culture by enjoying its nutritious, exquisitely presented food, sleeping in traditional Japanese inns and dipping in hotsprings, all the while focusing on the places to which Bashō travelled in 1689 and where he wrote many of his memorable haiku. In addition to the historians who study language change, and the haikuists who update season words, Matsuo Bashō's influence on haiku remains constant and sustainable.

References

Barnhill, D.L. (2005). *Bashō's journey: The literary prose of Matsuo Bashō*, translated and with an introduction. Albany, State University of New York Press.

Blyth, R. (1949). *Haiku* volume 1. Hokuseido Press.

George, B. (2016). "In the footsteps of Bashō: small group travel in Japan with a focus on Japanese literature." *A Hundred Gourds* 5(3), p. 1.

Matsuo, B. (1966). *The narrow road to the deep north and other travel sketches*, [translated from the Japanese with an introduction by Nobuyuki Yuasa]. Penguin Books.

Matsuo, B. (1985). *Monkey's raincoat sarumino: Linked poetry of the Bashō school with haiku selections*[Mayhew trans.], Charles E. Tuttle Company, p. 53.

Uedo, M. (1992). *Bashō and his interpreters: Selected hokku with commentary*. Stanford University Press.

Wawrytko, S. (2013). "Aesthetic principles of epistemological awakening: Bi and Xing in Bashō's haiku pedagogy." *Interculturalism and Philosophic Discourse: Retrospect and Prospect*, [ed. Y. Escande]. Cambridge.

Zolbrod, L. M. (1982). *Haiku painting*. Kodansha International, 1982.

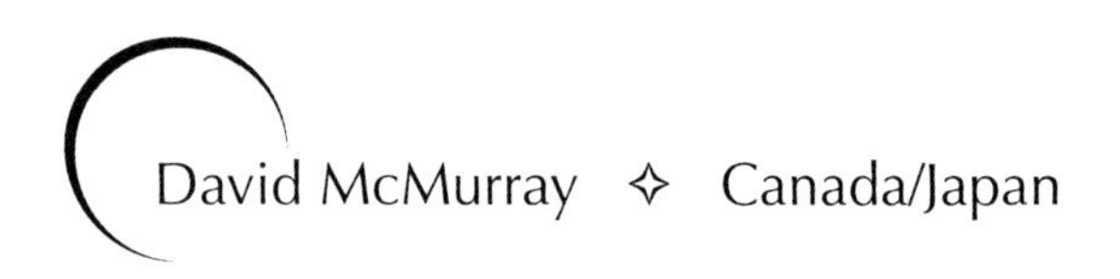

David McMurray ✧ Canada/Japan

When Love for War Poetry Fades

In World War 2, in Japan, special attack units were formed. It is rare to find citations in Japanese news or poetry today that refer to these sorties as suicide missions. Instead, the pilots were said to be following the special attack strategy of crashing or ramming their warplanes into enemy warships. The term *kamikaze* is often used by non-Japanese for Japanese fighter pilots who were sent on suicide missions. The name kamikaze literally and more poetically translates as divine wind. The names of the four sub-units within the Divine Wind Special Attack Force were: Unit Yamato, Unit Shikishima, Unit Asahi, and Unit Yamazakura. These names were adopted from a patriotic death poem, penned in 5-7-5-7-7 syllable form by the Japanese classical scholar Motoori Norinaga (1730 – 1801). His traditional tanka poem reads:

Shikishima no
yamato-gokoro wo
hito towaba
asahi ni niou
yamazakura bana

When arranged in a 5-7-5-7-7 syllable form, the translation could be:

> If someone would ask
> about the soul of Japan
> I would have to say,
> it is wild cherry blossoms
> glowing in the morning sun

Poetry by Soseki Natsume (1867 – 1916) provides an example of modern haiku penned by a teacher with war experience on an overseas excursion. He was an accomplished novelist and English teacher in Ehime and Kumamoto. His later writings reflected his views of the Russo-Japanese War (1904 – 1905). He penned this haiku in 1902 while he was studying abroad in London and received news that his colleague Masaoka Shiki (1867 – 1902) had passed away on September 19 (Keene, 2016). Shiki had served in the First Sino-Japanese War (1894 – 1895) as a war-correspondent until he became ill, returned to Japan and spent the rest of his life in bed coughing up blood.

> See how it hovers
> In these streets of yellow fog
> A human shadow

Under the summer clouds at Chiran Peace Museum beside a replica fighter plane in front of a bronze statue titled "Eternally," I found two World War 2 senryu verses. One was by a 19-year old pilot from Tottori and the other was from Hokkaido. The two phrases of senryu are both spectacular. The pilots' brushstrokes seem to have been made with a calm hand. Prior to their final sortie, these pilots wrote poetry for the sake of their homeland, their family, friends and loved ones. Although the young pilots must have died in agony, they left behind sincere thoughts and prayers of hope to find peace in heaven forever.

The second senryu poem arranged in 5-7-5 syllables without a season word reads:

> Come back from the dead
> My father just said one word
> That I had just said

This senryu poem deified a fighter plane, when translated, reads:

> The nose is lowered
> the body that becomes god
> is becoming straight

The following anonymous longer modern poem penned in three verses was on display at the Chiran Peace Museum and can be translated as a 5-7-5-7-7 syllable tanka in English.

The brave warrior
became a firefly light
we can keep in touch
with him through our five senses
at this festival on land

References

Keene, D. (2016). *The Winter Sun Shines in: A life of Masaoka Shiki*. Columbia University Press.

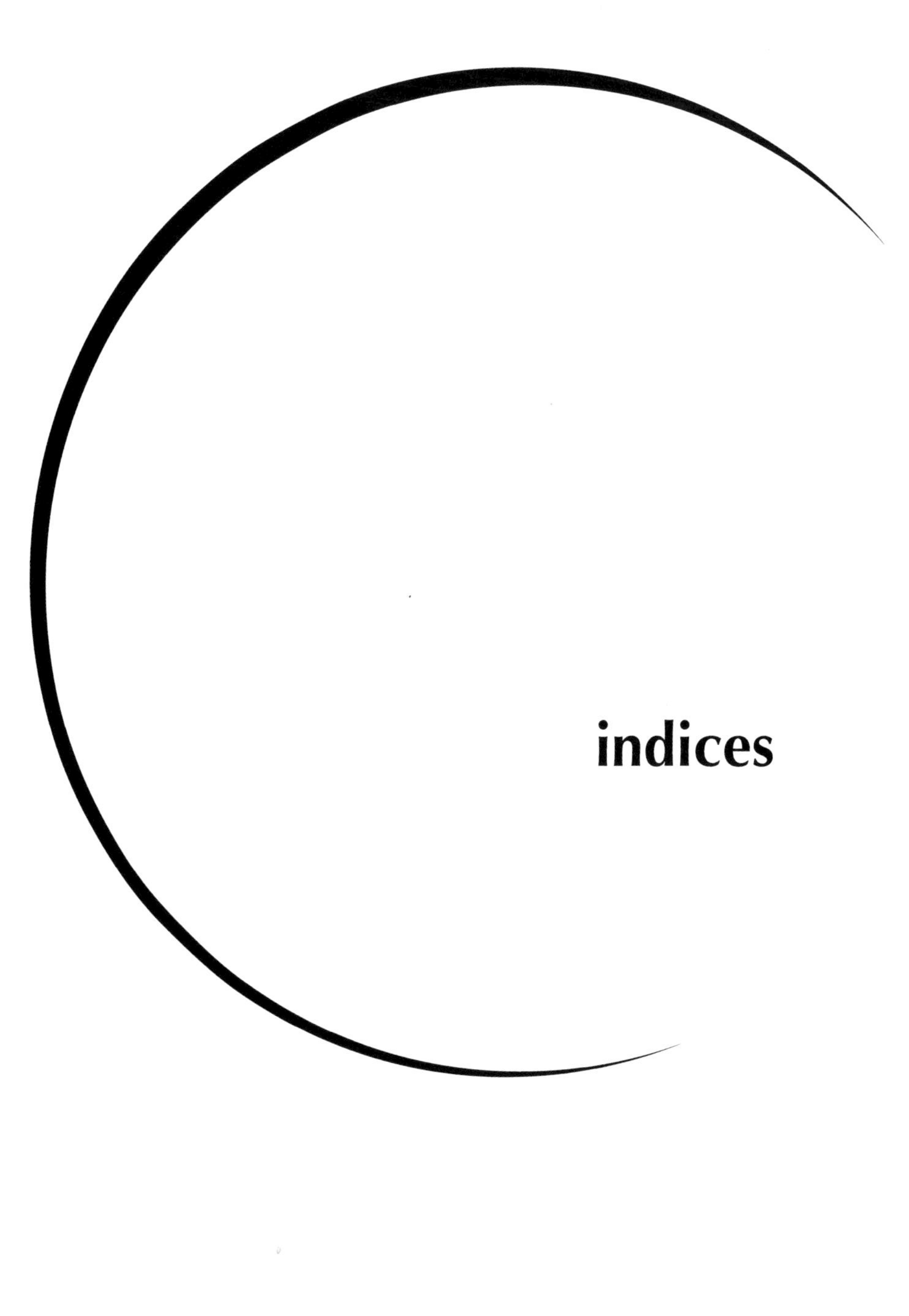

indices

index of authors

acknowledgments

Ahern—"until I hear" *AC* 49; **Anand**—"summer solstice" *MH* 53.1; **angela**—"after all" *HR* 138; **Antolin**—"night wind" *MA* 46, "the year ending" *UD* 2022/1, "uncut pomegranate" *MA* 46; **Arima**—"Haiku to Contribute" *HI* 155; **Arnold**—"airport taxi" *FF* 4; **Ashbaugh**—"Inheritance" *FM* 34, "jumping" AUS; **Ashraf**—"night in a forest" *SD* 65; **Austin**—"again he checks" *KK* 36; **Baker**—"an old pond" *SH* 47; **Balistreri**—"trying" *WP* 2; **Banwarth**— "newborn's death date" *FP* 45.2; **Basist**—"mother's day" *PR* 73; **Baysinger**—"not there" *FP* 45.2; **Beary**—"forsythia" *SS* 8, "What the Magdalene Asylum Scrubbed Clean" *BS* 32.1; **Bedi**—"pandemic" *CX* 55; **Bell**—"Glass Half-Full" *MH* 53.1; **Bennett**—"Euphony in Haiku" *MH* 53.1, "the sky" *AC* 49; **Bingham**—"an apology" *BS* 32.2; **Black**—"call to prayer" *BS* 32.2; **Blizzard**—"(Un)growing Up" *FM* 33; **Bold**—"divorce papers" *FP* 45.3; **Bowman**—"a stone child" *MH* 53.2; **Brooks**—"dark side of the moon" *HR* 140; **Burch**—"My Husband Laughs" *HK* 14; **Burfield**—"marriage breaking" *MH* 53.2; **Burgevin**—"afternoon moon" *MH* 53.1; **Burleigh**—"Haiku: Who's Counting?" *MH* 53.2; **Calvin**—"skipping stones" *SD* 64; **Camargo**—"covid moon" *MH* 53.1; **Campbell**—"Casting Couch" *DS* 17, "window shopping" *MF* 72; **Carson**—"a murmuration of snow" *SS* 8; **Chambers**—"a child's drawing" *BS* 32.3; **Chaturvedi**—"accompanying our dog" *AS* 29, "The Green Zone" *CH* 18.1; **Cheung**—"after the night shift" *AC* 48; **Chittaluri**—"climate change" AUS; **Ciobîcă**—"mayfly nymph" HHL; **Clement**—"retirement" *HN* 29.3; **Coats**—"enough to cover" *AC* 48; **Colgan**—"drinking alone" *MH* 53.3; **Courtney**—"night migration" *WP* 2; **Crocket**—"Nightfall" *DS* 14; **Cruz**—"my assigned gender" *WP* 3; **Curtis**—"binge watching" *AC* 48; **Day**—"amaryllis wombs" *WP* 4; **Dietrich**—"i am" *FP* 45.2; **Dobb**—"rural dawn" *ET* 2.1; **Doleman**—"The Right Way" *MH* 53.1; **Drouilhet**—"winter tree" *FP* 45.1; **Dudley**—"muddy March" *Haiku Zbornik* 25; **Dunstone**—"winter bonfire" *BS* 32.1; **Dutt**—"blood moon" *HK* 5; **Eklund-Cheong**—"mist on the river" *BS* 32.1; **Engel**—"two-day bus ride" *TD* 9; **Evetts**—"autumn leaves" *SB* 22; **Eyre**—"compost" *SD* 60; **Fay**—"the moment I know" *FP* 45.3; **Fischer**—"old ghosts" *WJ* Spring22; **Fleming**—"When Candy Bars" *PR* 72; **Ford**—"pitting" *BO* 23; **French**—"counseling session" *FP* 45.2, "The Red Sweater" *PR* 72; **Gaa**—"growing smaller" *AC* 49; **Gardiner**—"when there's no one left" *UB* 15sep22; **Gonzalez**—"family reunion" *BS* 32.2; **Gorman**—"custody hearing" *PR* 72; **Grant**—"prison gardener" *BS* 32.2, "your lawyer" *MH* 53.1; **Gurga**—"catch" *MA* 46; **Gwin**—"flecks of spring rain" *HR* 139; **Hall**—"finding a way" *BS* 32.2, "Into the Light" *BS* 32.2; **Hart**—"a woman" *HK* 9; **Hepworth**—"Chance Meeting" *HK* 10, "Fresh Start" *HK* 12; **Higgins, E**—"Van Gogh's Ear" *MH* 53.2; **Higgins, F**—"Manzanar" *MH* 53.2; **Holzer**—"sharing" *SD* 62; **Hooven**—"stray dog" *PR* 74; **Hotham**—"louder" *MH* 53.3, "news" *BS* 32.3, "whatever" *FP* 45.1; **Huddleston**—"new therapist" *MH* 53.2; **Hudspeth**—"kayak river tour" *WJ* Autumn22; **Jacobs**—"low winter sun" *MD* Feb22; **Jacobson**—"metal bracelet" *PU* 26 Aug22; **Kacian**—"a last scattering" *WP* 2, "every night" *CH* 18.1,"scars from scrapes" *FP* 45.2, "The Colonies" *MH* 53.1, "tracking your path" *FP* 45.1; **Keckler**—"Auschwitz tourists" *MH* 52.2; **Kelly**—"burnt forest" *BS* 32.4; **Kelsey**—"rising fog" KUS; **Kenney**—"careful" *FP* 45.3; **King**—"slow afternoon" *BS* 32.1; **Kingston**—"identity crisis" *HK* 11; **Latham**—"bone moon" *MH* 53.2; **Laurila**—"family reunion" *TW* 22.1; **Lee**—"tai chi" *BR* 47; **Lehmann**—"The Next Day" *PR* 74; **Lindquist**—"a long letter" *BS* 32.2, "April wind" *MP* 46, "green blackberries" *AC* 49; **Lucky**—"spring cleaning" *MH* 53.1; **m.**—"mother's room" *KF* 5, "suspecting mine" DRE; **Machmiller**—"the magnolia" *KF* 6; **MacRury**—"used book" *THF* 21Apr2022; **Mah**—"before the rain" *MF* 72; **Mahoney**—"Mom's labored breath" *AC* 48; **Mair**—"brief obituary" *KK* 36; **Makino**—"Covid variant" *MP* 46; **Maretić**—"dusty cloud" *THF* 31Aug2022; **Markworth**—"my life" *BO* 23; **Mason**—"snowmelt" POL; **McCormack**—"brushstrokes" *MF* 72; **McDonald**—"encrypted snow" *MP* 46, "Take Me Out" *MH* 53.3; **McGregor**—"epitaph" *HR* 138; **McKinley**—"new year calendar" *MH* 53.2; **McManus**—"night light" *AC* 48; **McMurray**—"light echoes across" *Haiku Down Under*, "Matsuo Basho" *TF* 23.3, "When Love" *TF* 23.2; **Metzler**—"the lone star" *FM* 33; **Miller**—"wildlife sign" *CX* 57; **Moldovan**—"autumn haze" *WJ* Autumn22; **Momoi**—"winter dusk" *PR* 72, "winter stars" *MH* 53.2; **Morcom**—"assisted living" *WP* 5; **Morrissey**—"old storybook" *MH* 53.1; **Nair**—"buzzing flies" *HK* 9; **Newson**—"grieving" *FP* 45.3; **Newton**—"museum bone flute" *AC* 48; **Ningthouja**—"the space between stars" *TH* 55; **Nyitrai**—"the moon" *MH* 53.2; **O'Connor**—"Perfection" *PR* 74; **O'Sullivan**—"lilies of the valley" *PR* 73; **Oates**—"church play" *MH* 53.2; **Oblak**—"funeral procession" *MH* 53.1; **Odeh**—"setting sun" EMB; **Olson**—"she nibbles" *MH* 53.2; **Packer**—"foyer portraits" *PR* 72; **Painting**—"nothing settled" *MH* 53.2; **Parashar**—"custody battle" *MH* 53.1, "patchwork quilt" *HK* 5; **Pearce**—"curtain of rain" *MF* 72; **Peat**—"last orders" *PR* 74, "snow buries everything" *NO* 21&22; **Phillips**—"early sunset" *MF* 72; **Piko**—"cooking for one" *CX* 55; **Pliško**—"lonely evening" *Haiku Zbornik* 25; **Polette**—"Gossip" *HK* 10, "Letter from Basho" *CH* 18.1; **Powell, R**—"just the nose" *Stratified Layers*; **Powell, T**—"summer dusk" *BS* 32.2; **Pray**—"what you said" *MH* 53.2; **Proctor**—"spring morning" *PR* 74; **Redmond**—"autumn winds" *HN* 24.1; **Rehling**—"two boats" *Samobor* 22; **Rhutasel-Jones**—"church steeple" *MH* 53.1; **Rickert**—"all the cats" *BS* 32.2, "The Next Day" *PR* 74; **Rielly**—"reading obituaries" *MH* 53.2; **Robinson**—"small town diner" *MF* 73; **Rodman**—"distant thunder" *MH* 53.2; **Root-Bernstein**—"spring morning" *BS* 32.2; **Salzer**—"finally" *FP* 45.1; **Sambangi**—"online dating" *WH* Winter21/22; **Savich**—"my father says" *PR* 73; **Schilling**—"blazing sun" *TW* 21.2; **Schwartz**—"anniversary sex" *MH* 53.1; **Schwerin, D.**—"if she floats" *WP* 5, "metal roof" *PR* 73, "we can't say" *WP* 3; **Schwerin, J.**—"carrying on" *AK* Summer22, "Easter morning" *SD* 63, "left behind" *MH* 53.2; **sekiro**—"buddha belly" *FP* 45.3; **Sexton**—"my mother asks" *ET* 9; **Shaw**—"trick or treat" *MH* 53.1; **Shires**—"obituary" *BR* 46; **Shpychenko**—"quarantined city" *AH* 18Mar22; **Simpson**—"a blizzard of petals" *ET* 9; **Singh**—"dragonfly" *TD* 9; **Slomovits**—"sparks from the campfire" *MP* 46; **Smith**—"Queen Anne's lace" *MF* 72; **Stevens**—"the retirement plan" *FP* 45.1; **Stevenson**—"an honorable mention" *TD* 7; **Strang**—"lockdown" *KK* 37; **Strange**—"estuary light" LYU; **Summers**—"Easter Monday" *THF* 17Apr22; **Tico**—"mansplaining" *TD* 7; **Toft**—"blue sky" *WJ* Winter22; **Tomczak**—"bedridden" *MF* 72; **van Helvoort**—"bedtime" *AH* 8May22; **Watts, D**—"after the funeral" *HR* 139; **Watts, L**—"Aberfan" *PR* 72, "Clocking Out" *MH* 53.2; **Wechselberger**—"family gathering" *PR* 72, "Unmasked" *FP* 44.2; **Welch**—"heirloom bowl" *FP* 44.1; **Wessels**—"ash-throated flycatcher" *UB* 2May22; **West**—"Endings" *DS* 15; **Willey**—"French word" *AH* 1Apr22; **Williams**—"morning news" *BS* 32.2; **Wilson**—"Quiet Corner" *BS* 32.1; **Wimberly**—"a gesture" *TD* 9; **windsor**—"child's grave" *BS* 32.3; **Witmer**—"a silent nightingale" *WP* 3; **Wynand**—"considering" *MH* 53.1.

cited sources

Books

Harrison, Carole (et al., eds.) — *Haiku Down Under Anthology* 2022 (Haiku Down Under, 2022)
Maretić, Tomislav (et al., eds.) — *Samobor Meeting* 22 (Matrix Croatica Samobor, 2022)
Montreuil, Michel (ed) — *Stratified Layers* (Haiku Canada, 2022)
Nazansky, Boris and Alenka Zorman (eds.) — *Haiku Zbornik* 25 (czkidn.hr/haiku-zbornik-2022)

Periodicals

AC — *Acorn* (ed Susan Antolin, acornhaiku.com)
BR — *bottle rockets* (ed Stanford M. Forrester, bottlerocketspress.com)
BS — *Blithe Spirit* (ed Caroline Skanne, britishhaikusociety.org.uk/journal)
FF — *First Frost* (ed Michael Dylan Welch et al., firstfrostpoetry.com)
FP — *Frogpond* (ed Jacob Salzer, hsa-haiku.org/frogpond)
HI — *Haiku International* (haiku-hia.com)
HR — *Hedgerow* (ed Caroline Skanne, hedgerowhaiku.com)
KF — *Kingfisher* (ed Tanya McDonald, kingfisherjournal.com)
KK — *Kokako* (eds Patricia Prime & Margaret Beverland, kokakonz@gmail.com)
MA — *Mariposa* (ed Carolyn Hall, hpnc.org/mariposa)
MF — *Mayfly* (ed Randy M. Brooks, brooksbookshaiku.com/mayfly)
MH — *Modern Haiku* (ed Paul Miller, modernhaiku.org)
PR — *Presence* (ed Ian Storr, haikupresence.org)
SS — *Seashores* (ed Gilles Fabre, haikuspirit.org/seashores)
TF — *The Field* (iuk.edu/field/the-journal)
TH — *Time Haiku* (ed Diana Webb, facebook.com/TimeHaiku)
UD — *Upstate Dim Sum* (ed Hilary Tann, upstate-dim-sum.com)

Contests

AUS — Australian Haiku Society Winter Solstice Haiku String (Australian Haiku Society)
DRE — Betty Drevniok Award (Haiku Canada)
EMB — Embassy of Japan Haiku Contest (Embassy of Japan)
HHL — Haiku Hike Literary Competition 2021 (Downtown Tucson Partnership)
KUS — Kusamakura Haiku Contest (Kumamoto University)
LYU — Maya Lyubenova International Haiku Contest (Bulgarian Haiku Society)
POL — Polish Haiku Contest 2021 (Polish Haiku Society)
THF — The Haiku Foundation Haiku Dialogue (The Haiku Foundation)

Online Sources

AK — *Akitsu Haiku Journal* (ed Robin White, wildgraces.com/Akitsu-Quarterly.html)
AS — *Asahi Haikuist Network* (ed David McMurray, asahi.com/ajw/special/haiku)
BO — *Bones* (ed Johannes S H Bjerg, bonesjournal.com)
CH — *contemporary haibun online* (ed Rich Youmans, contemporaryhaibunonline.com)
CX — *Creatrix* (ed Rose van Son et al, wapoets.com/creatrix)
DS — *drifting sands haibun* (ed Richard Grahn, drifting-sands-haibun.org)
ET — *Echidna Tracks* (ed Lyn Reeves, echidnatracks.com)
FM — *#FemkuMag* (ed Lithica Ann, femkumag.wixsite.com)
HK — *haikuKATHA* (ed Kala Ramesh, trivenihaikai.in)
HN — *The Heron's Nest* (ed John Stevenson, theheronsnest.com)
MD — *The Mainichi Daily* (mainichi.jp/english/haiku)
NO — *NOON* (ed Philip Rowland, noonpoetry.com)
PU — *Pulse* (ed Neal Whitman, pulse-journal.org)
SB — *Sonic Boom* (ed Shloka Shankar, sonicboomjournal.wixsite.com/sonicboom)
SD — *Stardust* (ed Valentina Ranaldi-Adams, stardusthaiku.blogspot.com)
SH — *Shamrock* (ed Anatoly Kudryavitsky, shamrockhaiku.com)
TD — *tsuri-dōrō* (ed Tony Pupello, tsuridoro.org)
TW — *tinywords* (ed Kathe Palka/Peter Newton, tinywords.com)
UB — *Under the Basho* (ed Don Baird, underthebasho.com)
WH — *World Haiku Review* (ed Susumu Takeguchi, worldhaikureview.wordpress.com)
WJ — *Wales Haiku Journal* (ed Paul Chambers, waleshaikujournal.com)
WP — *whiptail* (eds Robin Smith & Kat Lehmann, whiptailjournal.com)

The RMA Editorial Staff

Jim Kacian (1996) is founder of The Haiku Foundation, owner of Red Moon Press, and author of more than a score of books of and on haiku.

Francine Banwarth (2018) is past editor of *Frogpond* and coauthor, with Michele Root-Bernstein, of *The Haiku Life*, published in 2017.

Randy M. Brooks (2005) teaches haiku and other courses at Millikin University, edits *Mayfly*, and runs Brooks Books with wife Shirley.

LeRoy Gorman (2008) is the author of two dozen poetry books and chapbooks. He is past editor of *Haiku Canada Review.*

Maureen Virginia Gorman (1997) believes her study of haiku is a perfect complement to her work as a psychotherapist.

Gary Hotham (2014) is always alert for great English-language haiku. Latest chapbook, *Playground Grass: Haiku Options* (2022).

David Jacobs (2019) has won awards in both haiku and mainstream poetry. His most recent collection is *Buzz* (Red Moon Press, 2018).

Tomislav Maretić (2022) is the author of several haiku collections and his poems appear in several anthologies in both English and Croatian.

David McMurray (2017) authored *Teaching and Learning Haiku in English* (2022), and edits *Asahi Haikuist Network* in Japan.

Julie Schwerin (2017) is an associate editor at *The Heron's Nest* and curator of the Forest Haiku Walk.

Sandra Simpson (2012) is editor of the online *Haiku NewZ* and her own blog, *breath*. Her garden is a haiku in progress.

RMA Editors-Emeritus: **Dimitar Anakiev** (2000 – 2001), **John Barlow** (2007 – 2010), **Roberta Beary** (2007 – 2013), **Ernest J. Berry** (2002 – 2011), **Janice Bostok** (1996 – 2001), **Tom Clausen** (1996 – 2004), **David Cobb** (2004), **Ellen Compton** (1996 – 2002), **Cherie Hunter Day** (2013 – 2017), **Claire Everett** (2017 – 2018), **Dee Evetts** (1996 – 2001, 2003 – 2012), **Caroline Gourlay** (2005), **Lee Gurga** (1998), **Carolyn Hall** (2004 – 2006), **Yvonne Hardenbrook** (1996 – 1998), **John Hudak** (1996 – 1997), **Martin Lucas** (2006), **Peggy Willis Lyles** (2006 – 2010), **A. C. Missias** (2001 – 2005), **Emiko Miyashita** (2015 – 2016), **H. F. Noyes** (1996 – 1999), **Matthew Paul** (2012 – 2016), **Francine Porad** (1996), **Kohjin Sakamoto** (1997-2016), **John Stevenson** (2010 – 2016), **Ebba Story** (1996), **Alan Summers** (2000 – 2005), **George Swede** (2000 – 2007), **Dietmar Tauchner** (2013 – 2021), **Max Verhart** (2002 – 2012), **Jeff Witkin** (1996 – 2000).

The RMA Process

During the 12-month period December 15, 2021 through December 15, 2022, more than 3000 haiku and related works by over 2000 different authors have been nominated for inclusion in *skipping stones: The Red Moon Anthology* 2022 by our staff of 11 editors, as well as current journal editors, from hundreds of sources from around the world. These sources are, in the main, the many haiku books and journals published in English, as well as the internet. Editors are assigned a list of books and journals, but are free to nominate any work, from any source, they feel is of exceptional skill. In addition, the editor-in-chief is responsible for reading all of these sources, which ensures every possible source is examined by at least two nominating persons.

Editors may neither nominate nor vote for their own work.

Contest winners, runners-up and honorable mentions are automatically nominated.

When the nominating period concludes, all haiku and related works which receive nomination are placed (anonymously) on a roster. The roster is then returned to the editors, who vote for those works they consider worthy of inclusion. At least 5 votes (of the 10 editors, or 50% — the editor-in-chief does not have a vote at this stage) are necessary for inclusion in the volume. The work of editors must also receive at least 5 votes from the other 9 editors (55%) to merit inclusion.

The editor-in-chief then compiles these works, seeks permissions to reprint, and assembles them into the final anthology.